D0836639

JAY GRELEN'S
SWEET TEA TIMES

Volume I, Edition I

Sweet Tea Times, Volume I, Edition I by Jay Grelen, © 2014 by Jay Grelen's Storytelling, Sweet Tea and Housewashing Society, P.O. Box 13536, Maumelle, Arkansas 72113. Except where noted, the columns in *Sweet Tea Times* previously appeared in the *Arkansas Democrat-Gazette*, a copyrighted newspaper publication of Arkansas Democrat Gazette, Inc. 121 Capitol Avenue, Little Rock, Arkansas 72201, and are reprinted with the generous permission of Walter E. Hussman Jr., Publisher. All rights reserved. No part of this book may be used or reproduced in any manner without written permission except for brief quotations used in articles and reviews.

Except where noted, photographs in *Sweet Tea Times* were provided from private family collections and are © 2014.

Cover design: Advertising Design, Rowlett, Texas

Book design: Julie Grelen

Cartoons by John Deering, Editorial Cartoonist, Illustrator, *Arkansas Democrat-Gazette*, sculptor

Back cover photograph by Steve Keesee

Photograph of Little Rock 9 Monument on Page 113 © 2005 by Karen E. Segrave; *Testament,* the monument in the photograph, by John Deering

Royal Typewriter photograph by Ben Krain.

Sweet Tea column logo by Kirk Montgomery, Assistant Managing Editor/Design & Graphics, *Arkansas Democrat-Gazette*

Column photograph by Rick McFarland, Photographer, *Arkansas Democrat-Gazette*

First Edition, March 31, 2014

ISBN 978-0-9702362-9-6

Steve Keesee took the back-cover photograph of KTHV anchor Craig O'Neill at the moment a 4,000 pounds-per-square-inch jet of water drilled through the apple Craig was holding atop his head. Craig was part of the entertainment at the Albert Pike Hotel at the ribbon cutting for Jay Grelen's Storytelling, Sweet Tea and Housewashing Society. Tom Hopkins provided the barbecue for the Little Rock Regional Chamber of Commerce event in July 2011. Frankie Clay, whose story I tell in Sweet Tea Times, is the man in the bottom left corner of the photo.

For Sloane
Without whom …

It's britches, y'all

Jay Grelen writes like people from the South think and talk. No translation is needed as is often the case with writers educated in moss-covered institutions of the Ivy League.

Not that writers from those places can't communicate, but they really don't understand cornbread, purple hull peas, fried catfish, green-fried tomatoes, or Jay's signature recipe for sweet tea. Nothing against Lobster Newburgh, but it can't hold a candle to crawfish pie or shrimp and grits, and Jay understands that.

His writings in his beloved column "Sweet Tea" in the *Arkansas Democrat-Gazette* were must reads for the people of Arkansas who needed in their daily digest something other than Razorback sports, obituaries, and a list of which politicians had been arrested.

His columns evoke images of great Southern characters, food, culture and customs. He captures the heart and soul of the true Southern hospitality and gentility that has danged near been ruined by a bunch of outsiders who have moved in to enjoy the good life and who weren't properly brought up to appreciate that in the South people wear britches, not pants; they eat supper at night, dinner is at noon; and dogs ride in the cab of the pickup, children in the back.

~ Governor Mike Huckabee
Great State of Arkansas

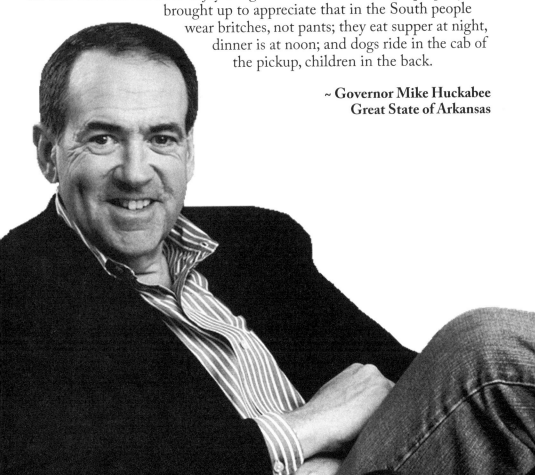

Never Heard of Him

Each of the columns in the *Arkansas Democrat-Gazette* had a cute little name, and so, therefore, would my column. My name by itself, the name my parents gave me, wasn't famous enough to reel in readers. Whoever heard of me? So late in the summer of 2004, as the debut of my column loomed, my boss and I spent the better part of a long time selecting a name.

This wasn't the first time. I've toiled in the newspaper racket for a while, and I've written columns for a slew of fine newspapers. I have run through a number of cute column names, all the way back to *The Tech Talk*, Louisiana Tech's student newspaper, where the editors called my column "Over the Fence." At the *Shreveport Times* in Louisiana, Lynn Stewart called my column "Grassroots." Stan Tiner, who took me on board at the *Mobile Register* in Alabama, was happy to stay simple with just "Jay Grelen." But when Stan took me to the *Daily Oklahoman* with him in 1999, he fell prey to the trend – he called my column "Down the Road." Carolyn Murray, an editor at *The Sun-News* in Myrtle Beach, South Carolina, came up with the most fitting: "Jaywalking."

The names that Managing Editor David Bailey and I rejected have slipped the bonds of memory. But I well recall the moment when Mr. Bailey appeared at my desk to announce his inspiration: *We have been overlooking the obvious …* And he paused in that inimitable down-from-the-mountaintop way of his. Then: *Let's call it "Sweet Tea."*

And thus was the column christened, inspired by my love of the house wine of the South. So in August 2004, Mr. Bailey and Executive Editor Griffin Smith, with the blessing of Walter E. Hussman Jr., owner and publisher, oped off some prime acreage for me on Page 1-B, better known as the Arkansas Page.

I wrote three Sweet Tea columns a week over a seven-year stretch that ended in June 2011. Now I have collected a handful of them into this book. The search for columns to include in the *Sweet Tea Times* was a painful exercise on many levels. As I sifted through the thousand or so columns, I found, for instance, phrases or whole paragraphs that, with the distance between the writing and now, are quite incomprehensible. By which I mean I have no idea what I meant. For instance: "The insistent yields to a contentment – a contentment well won, contentment to leaven any lingering urgency." It sounded good when I wrote it.

To cut down on your pain and suffering, I have either hammered out those incomprehensible musings, or, as in the case of the aforementioned inanity, scrapped them altogether.

Thank you for reading. Drink more sweet tea.

~ **Jay Grelen, Maumelle, Arkansas**
March 20, 2014

You have your Johnny Chapman, who went to (apple) seed, and you have your Johnny Sweet Tea (motto: Life is short, sugar is cheap, and sweet tea is fat free), whose real name is … Well, I am he.

My mission is to spread the gospel of Sweet Tea. *Southern Living* magazine, in fact, once referred to me as a "sweet-tea evangelist."

My love of sweet tea began at home in Pineville, Louisiana, where my two kid sisters and I were allowed a glass after supper after we had consumed our milk, which one summer wasn't easy. That summer, my mother, in an effort to economize, mixed our Foremost homogenized milk half-and-half with nonfat instant powdered milk. We called it "mixed milk," and it was awful, especially after it got warm in the glass, which it always did because I always put off drinking it.

My mother's sweet tea, though, was as good as the quote-unquote milk was awful.

When I worked for Stan Tiner at the *Mobile Register* in Mobile, Alabama, I rhapsodized in a column that sweet tea embodies all that is good about the South.

Readers rhapsodized back, which led Stan to suggest we sponsor a contest to find the best homemade sweet tea in South Alabama. So for the next five years, we held a contest every summer.

Rick Bragg wrote a story for *The New York Times* about my crusade to save the sweet-tea tradition. Rick, who grew up in Possum Trot, Alabama, where mamas keep sweet tea in gallon pickle jars, understood the significance.

"In a region where the summertime air is thick and hot and still even when it's dark," Rick wrote, "where people work hard and sweat rivers, hot tea was senseless and unsweetened tea was just brown ice water . ... Sweet iced tea spanned race and class; it was one thing Southerners had in common, besides mosquitoes and creeping mildew."

The work of a sweet-tea evangelist is not easy. In Oklahoma, for instance, the restaurants that serve the tea sweet are few and far between. Grits are hard to find, too, and once in a small-town diner, when I asked for rice to put under my pinto beans, the waitress looked at me as if I had ordered a bowl of dirt.

Arkansas isn't as uncivilized (sweet tea puts the civil in civilized) as Oklahoma, but I have some work to do. Too often, when I have asked a waitress for sweet tea, the answer has been: "Sweet'ner's on the table, sugar."

I should stipulate here that sweet tea and sweetened tea aren't the same. Sweetened tea may not be sweet enough. You must cross a certain immeasurable threshold with a batch of tea to accurately call it sweet. I can't tell you how to find it, but you will know it when you do.

Some have suggested that I spend too much time talking and thinking about and drinking tea. Well, I'm a Southern Baptist. I can't drink, cuss, dance, gamble or go to Disney World. What's left?

· · · · ·

In the film version of *Steel Magnolias*, Dolly Parton's character declared that iced tea is the "house wine of the South," a story with roots right here in the Natural State.

We can't say for certain who coined the "house wine" phrase or when, but you can find it in countless books and newspaper and magazine articles. But we have established with some certainty how the phrase made it into the script for the film version of *Steel Magnolias*, which originally was a play.

Robert Harling, the Southerner who wrote *Steel Magnolias*, spent some of his formative years in Natchitoches, Louisiana. He based the story on events in the life of his family. The moviemakers filmed *Steel Magnolias* in Natchitoches, home of the Christmas fireworks display on the Cane River.

Jon Davies, who lives in Little Rock, called this story to my attention. Jon is a cousin of Richard Davies, executive director of Arkansas Department of Parks and Tourism, who is at the center of this legend.

Since my attempt to contact Mr. Harling failed, we will rely on the ear-witness testimony of Jon Davies, who says it happened a long, long time ago atop a famous peak right here in the Land of Opportunity.

"Another cousin of ours, Liz Cravens, was married on Petit Jean Mountain," Jon wrote in an email. "The rehearsal dinner was at Mather Lodge."

She was engaged to Richard Harling, brother of the playwright.

"When the time came for toasts, Richard stood and, since alcohol was not allowed at the lodge, asked everyone to lift their iced tea, 'the house wine of the South.'

"The groom's brother is Robert Harling. During the laughter over Richard's one-liner, Robert was spotted pulling a notebook from his pocket and making a note.

"When the movie came out, I was listening for the line, and sure enough, there it was. This wedding took place after the play had been produced, so that's why you won't find the line in the play. I never asked Richard if he coined the line or repeated it, but it was new to me."

Any time you contact someone who writes for a newspaper, the way Jon did, you run the risk that the writer may actually respond and ask to put your name in the newspaper.

Which I did.

Not only was Jon agreeable, but he conducted his own little investigation to see whether he could determine the genesis of the phrase. Jon contacted his cousin Liz, who asked her brother-in-law, the playwright, about it.

"He had heard the line before," Jon wrote, "but Richard's use of it brought it freshly to mind, and that's how it got in the script."

· · · · ·

I have never paid money for sweet tea from McDonald's, where the beverage is simply another stream of revenue.

McDonald's, bless its French-fried Quarter-Pounder heart, has made sweet tea a nationwide household name, all well and good. But not in my house.

Sweet tea has been a staple in my family, like rice or salt, a presence at least as far back as the day of my birth. All the while that Mama was pregnant with me, she had dreamed of an ice cream sundae. When the doctor in Marianna, Florida, had finished with the forceps, however, Mama didn't ask for ice cream. Mama requested tea.

Sweet tea, made right, is a dessert. I will choose an after-supper glass of tea over banana pudding, though I am not beyond going for broke and washing down pudding with a Mason jar of tea.

I am blessed with a Southern wife who knows the difference between sweet tea and tea that is merely sweetened, and Sloane wants Sweet Tea. This woman – who once said: "I love the way our kitchen smells when you make tea." – will steal my glass of tea right out of my hand. If she requests water with her meal, that means that she'll drink her sweet tea from my jar. (She thinks if she drinks my tea instead of filling up a glass of her own, the caffeine won't keep her awake.)

At our wedding at Immanuel Baptist Church in Little Rock, instead of champagne (see above; we're Baptist), we served Sweet Tea alongside the groom's cake. And we didn't just serve it. We properly exalted it by dispensing it from our Arthur Court Sweet Tea dispenser, a fancy glass container that sits inside a pewter grape-leaf stand. A fancy dispenser, of course, is brushing gold on the daffodil. Sweet Tea needs no enhancement.

Susan Clark Alexander, Sloane's matron of honor, a maiden from Magnolia who breathes with a Southern accent, refers to my sweet tea as a Southern elixir, a remedy for the troubled soul.

Like the July and August humidity that bind us in misery, Sweet Tea embraces us and binds us like an attic-fan breeze on a summer night.

I don't begrudge McDonald's its impulse to make a buck off the House Wine of the South, but as for me and my house, we will make our own Sweet Tea.

~ Excerpts from several columns and an essay in the July 2012 *Arkansas Life*

Blowin' in the Wind

Robert Moore was worried for the newly arrived Okie who was hanging clothes on the solar laundry-drying unit behind his newly purchased ninety-year-old farm house.

That Okie would have been me. The date would have been sometime after Thanksgiving 2001.

Robert and his wife Marie, schoolteachers both, lived behind us on the outskirts of Conway, South Carolina.

Robert is a South Carolinian of the computer age. Why anyone would hang perfectly good clothes outside where dust and grasshoppers cavort in beams of drying sunlight stumped him.

He crossed the narrow land bridge that traversed the shallow ditch between our yards and, after a close inspection of the hanging garments, he inquired: "You folks gonna buy a dryer?"

Even at the turn of the century, yea, even the millennium, and even out on the rural routes, some people assume the only reason you would hang your clothes outside is because you don't have a store-bought dryer.

But as with so many things in life for a sentimentalist like me, a clothesline, is more than a place to evaporate water from your britches.

The walk to the clothesline, for instance, is moderate exercise, and when you hang the clothes, you stretch a little, and you absorb a moderate dose of vitamin D from the sun..

Sheets and shirts aflap in the wind, whether on a clothesline or a wire fence next to the pasture, are art in motion.

Once your clothes, towels and sheets are dry, sun-dried laundry is a natural air freshener.

I come by my love of the clothesline honest, descending as I do from pioneers in the deployment of solar clothes drying units.

Mamadee's line in El Paso, Texas, where the humidity averages minus-three percent on wet days, was the most efficient unit in my experience. Papadee built it in their backyard, in the 1930s, next to their rock garage.

On a blustery ninety-degree day, which is just about any day from February 14 until October 31, a pair of dripping-wet adult-male blue jeans will dry in the time it takes to eat two spoons of pinto beans rolled up with grated Jack cheese in a freshly made flour tortilla.

In Bryan, Texas, my paternal grandmother hid her clothesline behind a privet hedge. It was there, as a five-or-so-year-old, I learned about fire ants. As I watched Grandma pin clothes to the lines, I was standing in a bed of those lit matches on legs, which soon distracted me from the laundry.

Down in Pineville, Louisiana, my mama has been drying clothes on her solar unit since 1964. Daddy special ordered one built of iron from a machine shop. It will stand until the next great awakening. Until Daddy plugged the round ends with Styrofoam, the cross-beams were a nesting place for small birds.

Farther south in Louisiana, I knew a woman who dried her clothes on a solar unit with a middle post, which looked like an umbrella with the skin ripped off. Any good breeze off the Gulf of Mexico would spin it round, so not only was it solar-powered, it was wind-powered too.

In my so-called adult years, I have owned four solar units, starting with a sorry aluminum outfit I bought from a hardware store in south Alabama. My clotheslines have improved through the years, and the one in my Arkansas backyard is a hall-of-famer.

Charles Stall, who lived across the highway from me in South Carolina, really didn't know what a solar unit looked like when I asked him to build me one to take to Arkansas. (He grew up in Ohio, although I don't think that explains how he survived to adulthood without seeing one.) Based on my description, though, he built a pair of clothesline posts from square iron, five-stringers, that will hold five, sometimes six loads of clothes and will repel a bulldozer.

Shirts and towels are flapping outside my window right now, clipped to the lines with some of the spring-loaded wooden clothespins that Mamadee used half-a-century ago in El Paso. The pins are weathered almost rock-hard by the desert sun. When I hung the laundry an hour ago, sentimental me enjoyed again the knowledge that my grandmother's DNA lives in these pins, passed to the third generation, and that I could get by without a homemade dryer. If I had to.

~ April 5, 2009

The Grill's Gone Cold

I'm not the first person to tell Vivian Shadden that I wouldn't have stopped at her store unless someone had told me that I oughta.

"It looks like a junk store," concedes Vivian, whose family has owned the hundred-year-old building about fifty years. "I've had a lot of people tell me that. Once they get inside and look at all the old antiques ... they 'ooh' and 'ahh.'"

A lot of the "oohs" and "ahhs," however, weren't about the decor. In Marvell, you spell Bar-B-Q like this: Shadden's.

Wayne and Vivian Shadden go way back. Their families lived across the highway from each other. Wayne joined the Navy, where he was a cook, served in Korea and married.

Vivian, a registered nurse, was home to visit her mother when she learned that Wayne was back and divorced. They married in 1964.

They took over the store in the mid-1970s while Wayne still worked for Mohawk. When Mohawk closed in 1979, he went into barbecue full time.

As Wayne perfected his technique, he and Vivian couldn't find a sauce worthy of Wayne's pork.

"Finally," Vivian says, "I just mixed my own."

Wayne, upon tasting it, declared: "Well this is it."

Vivian, then, had to remember exactly how she had made it.

"I'm a dumper," she says. "I don't measure anything."

She cooked the sauce twenty gallons to thirty gallons at a time and stored it in five-gallon pails.

As Wayne won barbecue competitions in Memphis, they found the sauce didn't last. So Vivian made it evenings after work and on her days off.

Arthritis forced her to retire and entrust the secret recipe to a company in Mississippi for bottling, which required her to finally quantify her recipe, which took a day of weighing and measuring.

They spent another day ensuring the new sauce maker could make it right, which took about four batches.

"I was sick of barbecue that day," she says.

• • • • •

Wayne Shadden died on May 21, 2010. For the first time in nearly forty years, his cooker went cold and stayed that way. I spoke to Vivian by telephone a month later.

"I've closed the store for now," says Vivian, seventy, who was seven years younger than Wayne. "I was trying to take care of him. I didn't realize how tired I was until he died."

She hopes to reopen, but if she doesn't in the near future, their son Bryan and daughter Melanie Moreland plan to return to Arkansas.

"Bryan has big plans," she says.

She will continue to sell the sauce, however, which they bottle in Memphis and is for sale at Food Giant and Hays in Helena-West Helena, J and J's in Marvell, and at Dockers Bar and Grill in Hot Springs.

Or you can buy it directly from Vivian, who was putting up tomatoes and corn when we talked.

"I have it here at the house," says Vivian. "Call me."

~ June 29, 2010

If you haven't already called, you're out of luck. Vivian has moved out of state.

Rex Nelson's GPS: Good Pork Sniffing

The guy with the camera, the one taking pictures of his food every time we sit down to eat, that's Gary Saunders, a self-made expert on home-cooked restaurant food.

The second guy is an Arkadelphia boy named Rex Nelson who, in an effort to improve his social standing, went from working as a newspaper reporter to working for Governor Mike Huckabee, and from there to a job with the federal government. (As you might guess from the trajectory of his career, Rex didn't do real well on standardized tests, either.)

The third person in this trio is me, your big-footed (size fourteen), sweet-tea-slurping correspondent.

Our mission: A tour of barbecue joints in the Mississippi Delta, the sort of places you likely wouldn't enter unless someone you trust took you there.

Gary and I were trusting Rex (in spite of his affiliation the federal government), who knows his way around a plate and who, in his job with the governor and with the Delta Regional Authority, has learned the Delta so well he can travel it with his eyes closed and his sniffer open: Rex has his own version of a navigational GPS — Good Pork Sniffing.

"Beef cannot be barbecue," decrees King Rex. "It's got to be pork."

Gary, whose paying job is as general manager of the Texas Copperheads, Houston's arena football team, is the proprietor and CEO (chief eating officer) of Dixie Dining, an Internet site dedicated to the joys of eating in Southern cafes and diners. His mottoes: "Put Some South in Your Mouth" and "May the Fork Be With You."

Rex suggested the pilgrimage, and so on a gray rain-sodden day, I drove, Rex navigated, and we met Gary in Poplar Grove, where we ate our first sandwich at J.R.'s BBQ , owned by John Nunn.

The next stop was Jones Bar-B-Q, a two story cinderblock building off the main drag in Marianna, where James H. Jones builds sandwiches in less than thirty seconds: He keeps a mound of pork under an aluminum pan, warmed by a heat lamp. He heaps the meat onto a slice of Wonder white bread, dollops on the slaw and hands it out a window into the dining room.

He's the fourth generation of his family to sell barbecue.

The day we were there, Sylvester Robinson was tending the fire out back in massive pits where he can smoke a thousand pounds of meat at a time. Gary rated the barbecue as good as any he has eaten in Memphis.

After Marianna, we made an unscheduled stop at Cypress Corner Bar-B-Q , between Marianna and Walnut Corner, that not even Rex had tried.

Dennis Jones smokes the meat there in the most modern-looking of the pits we saw. He learned to cook from a fellow named George Avant.

"I soaked up all I could from him," he says.

Next stop was Shadden's, which is on U.S. 49 west of Marvell. The furnishings include an old drink cooler that doesn't work. Shadden's won't sell beer or cigarettes on credit.

By this point in our tour, I was leaving the top half of my bun off my sandwich. We still had one more stop.

And that was Craig's in DeValls Bluff, which is Rex's favorite. (Gary had peeled off by now, but no slacker he, Gary found his fifth stop on his way to north Mississippi, where he lived until two weeks ago.)

"So much swine," Gary said in parting, "so little time!"

But we three made the most of our swine time — two-hundred-eighty miles and five pork sandwiches in about four hours. Considering the way we ate that day, we oughta name our route The Pig Trail. Oink.

~ March 7, 2007

Rex Nelson is president of Arkansas' Independent Colleges & Universities and the man behind Rex Nelson's Southern Fried at rexnelsonsouthernfried.com. Gary Saunders lives in Fairhope, Alabama, where he remains the Chief Eating Officer of Dixie Dining at dixiedining.com.

FORT SMITH — My lunch at Ed Walker's Drive In goes in my cornbread diary.

The October afternoon was autumn cool that day, which means cool with a touch of warmth, the way the hood on a car feels an hour after you park it in the shade. You could see clear through the blue to eternity.

T.J. Brown took me to Ed Walker's,

where, if you want service at your car, you park at the curb and flash your headlights.

T.J., who works on a heavy-bridge maintenance crew for the state, knows a lot of stuff and has done a lot of stuff. For years, he worked in the logging woods, where the money was good, the danger high.

On Friday, he was halfway through his Ed Walker hamburger when our conversation turned to cornbread. I'm not sure how that happened, except that it was one of those life moments meant to be a moment that, in retrospect, you knew was coming.

T.J. told me how he bakes cornbread. He learned the technique from his grandmother. And technique is the operative word. Technique is what elevates this cornbread.

Any good cornbread recipe will be better if you employ T.J.'s grandmother's technique:

First, pour three-fourths of a cup of vegetable oil into your cast-iron cornbread skillet, put it in the oven, and heat the oven to four-hundred-twenty-five degrees. It's important that you put in the skillet as soon as you turn on the oven. What you want to do is heat up the oil. Get it really hot.

While you wait for the oven to heat, mix your dry ingredients. (T.J., I am sorry to report, uses Aunt Jemima's self-rising cornmeal.) Stir your milk and egg into the dry ingredients at the last minute. Pour the batter into the skillet, slowly, because it's going to sizzle and spurt.

Spread the batter to the edge of the skillet and bake it for twenty minutes.

That was my lunch on Sunday. Nothing but steaming, crunchy, buttered (the real stuff, not margarine) cornbread. I baked a second batch for Tuesday. (Second time around, I cut the oil to half a cup.) Cornbread as supper is legal because cornbread meets the ol' ketchup-and-salsa-are-vegetables criteria. In cornbread, we have four of the food groups: two vegetables (corn and vegetable oil), dairy (milk in the batter, a quarter stick of butter per wedge), grain and protein. To round out the meal, I added a fifth food group, which, goes without saying, was the house wine of the South.

So there is how T.J. Brown's grandmother cooks the cornbread. Careful who you tell about this. Once the word is out, your cousins and neighbors will be parking in your driveway, flashing their headlights and demanding cornbread service.

~ **October 8, 2009**

GASSVILLE — Lurch isn't dead. Not even close. And Janice Wolf, his primary caregiver, isn't rushing him.

She winces, in fact, at the thought of it all. Lurch has lived with her since he was five weeks old.

But when you have a prize like Lurch, you don't leave the choice of a taxidermist until his dying breath. So Ms. Wolf has lined up one in Texas.

"I want to be sure people can see him years after he is gone," she says.

Ms. Wolf, who descends from early Arkansas settler Jacob Wolf, inherited an appropriate name for her avocation, which is the rescue of animals.

Ms. Wolf is Dr. Dolittle, Ellie May Clampett and Mother Teresa all wrapped into a blue shirt over flared jeans and flipflops.

Rocky Ridge Rescue, her Puddleby-on-the-Marsh, was a pile of rocks she rearranged into a home for her animals.

"I've rescued my whole life," she says. "Animals don't sit and whine about what happened to them. They get on with it."

Ms. Wolf rescues what she prefers to call "special-needs animals."

Tristan, missing a leg, Piper, blind in an eye, and Cornbread, who is deaf, are among her special-needs dogs. She had no hope for the blind and battered fawn someone left with her. But with Ms. Wolf's care, Lazarus has returned to sight and life, gentle and affectionate as a lamb. Lassie is a sheep who thinks she is a dog. Zebiscuit is a zebra she nursed to health.

"It's a group home," she says. "The rule is you've got to get along."

Lurch, oddly enough, wasn't a rescue but an impulse purchase in Missouri.

"He was a tiny baby," she says. "I went up to an exotic ranch to pick up a three-legged llama."

And she saw Lurch.

"Something told me I was supposed to have him. I talked them into selling him to me for three-hundred dollars."

Lurch is a Watusi, an African breed known as the Cattle of Kings. In Africa, ownership indicated status and wealth, if not royalty.

If a Watusi with normal-sized horns is fit for kings, kings might have killed for Lurch. Editors of the *Guinness Book of World Records* were impressed enough that they featured him in the 2005 anniversary edition.

Ellen DeGeneres was so impressed with Rocky Ridge Rescue that twice she sent film crews to Arkansas and broadcast Lurch's story on her show.

"He was a normal little baby," Ms. Wolf says. "I used to worry when he was little that his horns grew abnormally slow. He was a late bloomer."

But Lurch's horns grew. And grew. They are still growing. At last measure, their circumference at his head was thirty-eight inches. Each weighs about a hundred pounds. Tip to tip, they measure more than seven-and-a-half feet. In some pictures, Lurch's horns look like twisted pigtails sticking straight out.

Lurch, not exactly fierce in appearance, is gentle and protective. In his younger days — he is thirteen — children rode on his back and hung from his horns.

Ms. Wolf named him Lurch before she knew his destiny.

"He grew into his name," she says. "The one Watusi I get is the world record. No one can explain this. This is not normal."

~ December 9, 2008

Lurch died May 22, 2010.

To Bill and Hillary: Totally unintentional

HOPE — Barry Kemelhor would like to explain an honest misunderstanding to Bill and Hillary Clinton.

Barry and his wife, Karen, weren't trying to fool the First Couple that night at the inaugural ball. They simply were being neighborly.

But with twelve years to reflect upon the moment, they understand how it looked to the Clintons.

Mr. Kemelhor is hard-core Clinton. He and Karen came here from Rockville, Maryland, on what he calls a Billgrimage. They had tickets to the opening of the library, and they came down early and paid for a private tour of Hope, which is where I met them, with native Linda Howell and Jerri Wright, who works at Little Rock's Visitor Information Center.

On their visit to Clinton's haunts Monday, Mr. Kemelhor wore a vintage Clinton T-shirt, black, with a mug shot of Clinton, blue in the face, blowing on a saxophone. "The cure for the blues," says the T-shirt, a relic from the 1992 campaign.

Mr. Kemelhor reckons that Clinton, with his elephantine memory, probably recalls the incident in question, which occurred January 20, 1993, at Union Station, site of one of the president's inaugural balls.

Mr. Kemelhor's accountant gave them tickets to the ball after the woman the accountant had invited — a Republican, he discovered too late — declined. "I hate Bill Clinton," she told the surprised bean counter.

The Kemelhors arrived at four p.m. at Union Station, the first celebrants, by their account, in Washington, D.C.'s, storied train station. Mr. Kemelhor found two folding wooden chairs beneath stairs and set them up near the stage.

As the other guests arrived (eventually more than ten-thousand), two Filipino women staked their spot behind the Kemelhors. The two rather short women asked the Kemelhors to remain seated so they could take pictures of Clinton.

The Clintons arrived nearly eight hours later. As the band played "Hail to the Chief," the crowd was on its feet. Everyone but the Kemelhors, who kept their promise to the women behind them.

After a moment, the Clintons — to the astonishment and perplexity of the Kemelhors — personally greeted them.

"They were kneeling down. They were posing for our camera. They said, 'We appreciate you so much.' You know Bill can bite the lip," Mr. Kemelhor says. "It was amazing how nice they were being to us."

As the Clintons left, the Kemelhors stood to cheer. When Hillary saw them stand, her happy demeanor changed. "Hillary turned around and gave us this withering stare," Barry says.

After the unexpected attention, Barry and Karen were even more confused by the sudden turn in mood.

Much later, understanding dawned. The Clintons thought they had suckered them. "They thought we were handicapped," Mr. Kemelhor says.

The misunderstanding notwithstanding, the Kemelhors believed they learned something about the character of the couple, which is why he likes to tell the story.

"The lesson for me," Barry says, "was what kind and decent people they are."

• • • • •

Last we heard from hardcore Clinton fan Barry Kemelhor, which was just a couple of days ago, he and his wife, Karen, were in Hope, all the way from Rockville, Maryland, on what he called his Billgrimage.

Then comes the telephone call from Barry on Thursday, the Big Day, the reason they came to Arkansas, opening day for the Bill Clinton library.

Barry was calling from an emergency room while he awaited his turn under the X-ray machine.

To say Barry is hardcore Clinton understates his devotion. Barry and Karen had tickets to the library opening because he had bought a brick with his name on it that is part of the paving at the library. While they were in Hope, he bought a brick to support the Clinton birthplace. To see Hope, Barry paid for a private tour.

While they were in Hope, they met Edna Fielding, who remembers little Billy Blythe carrying his Bible to Sunday school. They toured the home where Clinton lived with his grandparents.

"You see where Bill Clinton came from, the store his grandfather ran, the only store that would extend credit to blacks," Barry said. "I know him a little better."

That was Monday. On Tuesday, they attended the Little Rock Regional Chamber of Commerce meeting to hear Bill's speech, and they saw Aretha Franklin's show at Robinson Center Music Hall.

On Wednesday, they attended the First Lady's luncheon so they could see Hillary. They ate at Doe's Eat Place and chatted with owner George Eldridge. They visited the Clinton Museum Store.

"We've bought everything you can buy," he said.

All of that, though, was busy work to occupy them until Thursday morning.

By six-forty-five a.m. Thursday, they had joined the throng of faithful snaking under Interstate 30 and onto the grounds of the William J. Clinton Presidential Center for the dedication. Barry wore a brown wool suit and carried a one-dollar plastic wrap for his head.

Then he tripped.

"It was some kind of a construction sign," he said, "the long legs [were] sticking out over the sidewalk. I put out my left arm to break my fall. I fell out into the street."

He showed his wrist to nearby paramedics, who iced it and proposed a ride to an emergency room.

They told him the round trip likely would take three hours. "I told them, 'I'm not going to miss Bill Clinton.'"

Nearly seven hours later, Barry and his wife took the ambulance ride to Baptist Health Medical Center. He left with a splint on his double-fractured wrist.

"I've never broken a bone in my life," he said. "I still have all my wisdom teeth. I don't want to exaggerate it, but it hurt."

He ripped his suit, too.

He couldn't take pictures, and since he couldn't clap, he slapped his right thigh.

The Kemelhors left Little Rock on Friday to visit Dallas so they could be there Monday for the anniversary of the assassination of JFK, Barry's other presidential idol. But he called Monday to say the pain forced them to cut their trip short.

All this rain and pain for Bill Clinton?

Bill Clinton, Barry is certain, would do as much for him.

· · · · ·

Back home, surgeons inserted twelve screws and a steel plate in his left wrist.

"I have a six-inch scar," he says. "That's a badge of honor."

Several months later, President Clinton wrote to Barry: "The dedication ceremony was an incredible experience for me, and I'm so glad you could be a part of it.

"I hope that by the time this reaches you, you are on the mend and your wrist is feeling better."

~ November 21 and 23, 2004

Best I can tell, Barry Kemelhor was the first person to utter the word "Billgrimage," at least for publication.

And you, gentle subscribers, were the first to read it, as the word first appeared in print right here in this space, put here by your big-footed correspondent, not once, but twice, in back-to-back columns in November 2004. (We claim our fame and significance where we can, and you were part of it.)

Six months later, in the spring of 2005, "Billgrimage" started showing up in newspapers and magazines whose writers had traveled to Hope, Hot Springs and/or Little Rock.

Barry, who earns his living playing with words, wants the credit.

"I should have patented it," says Barry, a writer who named his company Wordplay Inc. and who graduated, fittingly, from Walt Whitman High School. "I've seen it a number of times. It doesn't come up often anymore. It might [again] if Hillary gets the nomination."

Barry was a political science major who, at age seven, shook JFK's hand through the White House fence.

Barry, by my measure, has a legitimate and hard-won right to claim and to defend his coining of "Billgrimage."

On their Billgrimage, Barry and Karen found much to like in Arkansas, including the steaks at Doe's and Mama B's burgers, one of which Barry consumed on the way back to the hotel after his trip to the emergency room. He ate it with his right hand; his left was in a cast.

"We thought the people were fantastic," he said last week. "We never fail to mention Mama B's burger."

He came. He tripped. He made up a word.

~ July 8, 2007

In 2007, Mr. Kemelhor gave $2,300 to Hillary Clinton in support of her presidential campaign, according to the website campaignmoney.org. A point of interest: Barry's late father, Robert E. Kemelhor, helped develop the U.S. Navy's Polaris submarine missile program, according to the elder Kemelhor's March 16, 2011, obituary in The Washington Post.

The price of eating all you can at Pancho's

If you eat at a Pancho's all-you-can-eat Mexican buffet, don't worry that your hearty appetite will force the restaurant into financial ruin. Buford Suffridge, lover of Mexican food, heard it straight from Pancho himself.

First, his Mexican food biography: Buford, who grew up in Perryville in the 1940s and '50s, didn't taste Mexican food until he entered the University of Arkansas in the fall of 1958.

"I immediately fell in love with it," he wrote after he read about my love for it. The Mexican restaurant where he took his first bite, the name of which he can't recall, was near the airport on Highway 71. He often took his girlfriend — "now my wife, Lynda, of 42 years" — there.

During the summers of 1962, 1963 and 1965, when Buford worked as a park ranger for the National Park Service at Carlsbad Caverns in New Mexico, he made up for those eighteen enchilada-less years.

That was the summer that Buford discovered Pancho's, which originated in El Paso, Texas, my mother's hometown. El Paso was a hundred-forty miles away from Carlsbad Caverns.

"Since the highway was flat, wide, lightly traveled, lightly patrolled by the Texas Highway Patrol (who would not bother you as long as you kept it below 120 mph) and with only one curve ... at 90 mph [it] was not difficult to drive after work ... and return the same evening," Buford wrote. "Incidentally I still own the 1959 Ford Thunderbird I used many times for that trip."

Buford discovered Pancho's, thanks to one of his co-workers, who grew up in Carlsbad and knew the man who owned Pancho's — all you could eat for two-dollars and twenty-five cents.

"Needless to say, we immediately became enamored with this place, and to this day, Pancho's Mexican Buffet remains my all-time favorite Mexican restaurant."

So Buford tells the story of his first visit to the El Paso Pancho's, which involves his good friend George Cain, who "reports that the Pancho's in [Albuquerque] is doing an admirable job holding up the fine tradition."

"When he and I were young Park Service employees, we would fast for 24 hours before hitting the one in El Paso. The first time we ever went to eat there, we were with Bill Birdsell, the [park ranger] who knew the owner.

"George was coming back to the table with about his fifth plate piled high, and Bill said to the owner: 'You aren't going to make any money off this guy tonight.'

"To which the owner replied: 'There isn't a man alive who can eat two-dollars and twenty-five cents worth of this stuff.'"

~ **February 8, 2007**

PERRYVILLE — Buford Suffridge Sr. wanted Norman Rockwell to do his talking for him.

So Mr. Suffridge cut a Rockwell painting from his *Saturday Evening Post*, framed it and hung it in his office at his sawmill.

Breaking Home Ties showed a leathered man perched forlornly on the running board of his truck as his eager son prepared to leave home.

After Buford Sr. closed the sawmill, he moved the *Post* cover to an office behind their new house. Buford Sr. died in 1983, and these forty-six years later, the picture hangs right where he nailed it in 1963.

The *Saturday Evening Post* recently published a letter Buford wrote about his favorite cover: "Although my father has been dead for nearly 26 years, the September 25, 1954, cover of the *Saturday Evening Post*, complete with address label, still hangs within the homemade frame. ... At the time, I was almost 14 years old and thought it strange a man would cut the cover from a magazine ... and hang it in his office. ... Only as an adult with three sons of my own did the significance sink in. ...

"I came to realize how he dreaded the day when he, like the father in the cover, would sit with hat in hand as his only son prepared to leave the confines of home. ... Like my father, this gentleman came from a generation that never had the opportunity to experience what lay ahead for his son, and Mr. Rockwell perfectly captured on his face the helplessness ... and the sorrow of the dog that, like the boy's father, knew things were never to be the same again."

There was no Rockwellian moment in Buford Jr.'s real-life, departure for college. Buford, an orthodontist, found that prying emotion from his father that day was like pulling teeth. Buford, noticing his father hadn't cleaned up for the trip to

Fayetteville, said: "I thought you would go with me."

"I'm working."

"I don't even know how to get to Fayetteville," Buford said.

"Stop at Junior's Gulf station," said his father, "and pick up a road map."

Don't misunderstand, Buford says: "There was never any doubt that he loved me. He just never said it until just before he died."

Just before Buford and Lynda's oldest son left for the University of Arkansas, Buford remembered the Norman Rockwell cover that "spoke words I could never put into a sentence." He ordered three prints of *Breaking Home Ties*, framed each, and as each son left home for college, he gave him a copy.

"Although I don't recall that any of them really had much to say about it at the time, I think it eventually made the same impression on them that it did on me, because they all have it hanging in their office. And I didn't ask them to do that."

~ March 24, 2009

Love her was all he could do

Jack Dallas figured out that the wife was the troubled one, which is the sort of thing you learn about a husband and wife when they belly up to your supper table at your restaurant two or three times a week.

Jack Dallas didn't know right off that the wife was at the root of the couple's eccentricities.

But he observed and listened and came to understand that the man of their house simply didn't know how to fix his wife. So he tolerated the gardening gloves she wore everywhere and the bedsheet burning and the looks of people who didn't take the time to know them.

He loved her. He didn't need to fix her to love her.

They had sold their farm upstate and moved into the Albert Pike when it was a high-dollar downtown hotel. Some days they ate at Franke's, where she always chose a slice of pie from the back – because it was less likely to be germy – and several evenings a week they ate at Embers, the Little Rock steakhouse that Mr. Dallas and his brother bought in 1959.

The wife was, indeed, eccentric, Mr. Dallas recalls with evident affection.

"She inspected every glass just about in the restaurant before she picked out one she would use," says Mr. Dallas, who worked in a tuxedo. "She wore an old dress — a printed dress. Housecoat on top of that. And on top of that, a plastic raincoat.

"Brown stockings with house shoes. Hands covered with a pair of old brown garden gloves."

They had a regular waitress, whose car note they paid every month.

Once they bought an Oldsmobile in Little Rock, drove it straight into the Albert Pike parking garage, put it up on blocks and never drove it again. Instead, they hired a taxi for a day at a time, whether they were staying in Little Rock or traveling to Memphis or Hot Springs.

Over time, Mr. Dallas learned that the wife was terrified of germs. Her husband simply played along.

"Each day," Mr. Dallas says, "the taxi had to be fumigated. They insisted on having brand-new sheets every day. The sheets they took off their bed had to be burned. They kept linen departments in business.

"Apparently she trusted us enough to serve her food."

On every visit to the Embers, she purchased Camel cigarettes. "She would tear open the package and dump cigarettes into a brown paper sack. When she smoked after dinner, she did not wear her gloves."

Every morning a Union Bank messenger delivered their spending money. "It had to be brand-new money — couldn't be used."

Over the years, Mr. Dallas listened to them, which is why, of course, they ate supper with him, and that is how he figured out she was the troubled one, and that the root of the trouble was the death of their seven-year-old child, killed by a rare disease. So the wife, fleeing grief and regret and germs, buttoned her raincoat over her housecoat over her dress, sealing in the sadness, and dragging her dirty sleeves through the slices of cafeteria pie so she could have an uncontaminated slice from the back.

~ April 23, 2009

No thought for herself

If you know who you're looking for, you can find Claire Kane among the hundreds of runners in the photograph on Sunday's Arkansas page.

Lime green shirt, which identifies her as a Mount St. Mary student but still doesn't narrow it down much.

Second row of runners, pink headband, second from left. That isn't her, either. But look just to the right of the headband, and there she is, peeking out from the third row.

Staton Breidenthal snapped this picture for the *Arkansas Democrat–Gazette* at the start of the Susan Komen race before anybody knew what Claire would do afterward. Before Claire even knew.

Here's something to think about — four-hundred-ninety teenagers attend Mount St. Mary, and two-hundred-twelve of them showed up on Saturday morning to run three-point-one miles to raise money for breast-cancer research. Fourteen-year-old Claire was among that forty-three percent of the student body to run.

Claire, a freshman, is a member of the school's cross-country and track teams who rises before the sun to train with her teammates.

On Saturday, she finished first among her schoolmates and Number Fifteen out of the forty-five-thousand who ran.

Not Number Fifteen in her age group. Number Fifteen out of forty-five-thousand runners.

Her time, 21:47:41, was her fastest three-point-one mile ever and qualified her for a medal, which she wore for little more than the time it took her to win it.

After the race, she and friends who were strolling among the booths stopped to pose for a picture next to a portable restroom that was disguised as a pink milk carton. Or as Claire describes it: "A dressed-up porta-potty."

A woman approached them to ask about their times and to admire their medals. Claire isn't sure about this because the woman was wearing a jacket, but at the time she thought that the woman was wearing one of the pink shirts reserved for survivors of breast cancer.

The woman, in her thirties, told them that she had run a twenty-eight-minute race, not fast enough for a medal. She really wanted to win a medal, she told them.

So without time to even think, Claire removed her newly won medal from around her neck and gave it to the woman.

"I just kind of reached for it," she said when we visited in a conference room at Mount St. Mary.

The woman tried to refuse it, then accepted it. Then she cried. Then the woman's mother cried. Then they posed for a picture with Claire and her friends. Then they parted paths, and Claire returned home without her Five-K hardware on a pink Susan Komen strap.

Claire is the only daughter in a family of five: parents Tom and Rebecca; older brother Matthew and kid brother Max.

Chances are that this won't be the last time you'll see Claire Kane's name and photograph in this newspaper, this Mount St. Mary student and runner who is impulsively generous, instinctively kind.

~ **October 21, 2010**

Sure enough, not only did Claire's name show up in the newspaper again, I was writing about her again only three weeks later.

Shortly after noon on the last Tuesday of October, the all-girl student body reported to the gym for an unscheduled assembly for an unknown purpose.

Principal Diane Wolfe introduced Sherrye McBryde, Komen's Arkansas executive director, who praised the school's participation in the race, and noted that one student, in particular, through an act of particular compassion, exemplified what Race for the Cure is all about.

Claire's parents, Tom and Rebecca Kane, and Claire's grandparents Dan and Mary Jane Bailey, watched from the sidelines as the executive director invited a very surprised Claire to step front and center. Errin Dean, a Mount St. Mary graduate, looped a replacement medal around Claire's neck.

The way her four-hundred-something schoolmates hollered and clapped, you'd think Claire had set a cross-country world record. Claire, her face hinting at the strain of the attention, looked alternately at the floor, at her classmates and at her family. She unconsciously pawed the floor like a thoroughbred, a reflexively good, self-conscious colt about to bolt, this young woman whose example before her peers gives peer pressure a good name.

~ **November 7, 2010**

Madie

She ran, Madie did, three short quick new-born-calf steps downhill toward the swings.

She was ahead of me. Then she remembered I was with her and slowed. She didn't say anything, didn't look back. But I knew why she let off the gas.

Madie is thoughtful like that, thoughtful beyond her sixteen years.

"No, go," I said. "Run."

So she ran to the swings, and before I slow-footed the distance between the swings and me, Madie was airborne, the chains, and the hooks that hold the chains, squawking and honking like a goose overhead. A goose or two.

The park, of course, was Madie's idea. We had been standing in the auditorium at her school, Madie, her mother and me, after the character assembly. (Word for Today: Patriotism. Madie was one of the cheerleaders, and she was front and center, which, in my opinion, makes her head cheerleader.)

The day is nice, Madie observed to us. And paused. Then phrase by phrase, she asked: "Think we. Could go to. The park?"

And, of course, we could, Madie and me, just us, because other duties demanded Mom's presence elsewhere.

Sixty degrees on this day in mid-January, a day and a moment that as easily could pass for the first day of spring. A day for a swing.

Madie's love of swings is legendary in the family. From the time she could sit up and swing, she has swung. Hours, her family says.

This, though, was my first sight of Madie actually swinging. To see Madie swing was more of a vision, by which I mean I felt as though I was watching a holy union, a sacred ritual, between Madie and the universe.

This is what I saw: First, her face. Rapture and bliss each is an apt description but insufficient; each adjective only describes what we see on the outside.

Madie's face speaks of something only Madie can know. There is a rhythm, an unconscious method, it seems, to Madie's transport.

At the height of her backswing, Madie puts each hand to the chain, more to guide it than to hold it. As the swing falls to the lowest position, she moves her hands toward each other until the chains stop her arms at the inside of her elbows, and her arms cross in front of her midriff. On the upswing, then, she pulls slightly on the chain, which, apparently, is the motion that keeps her swing swinging.

Finally, on the backwards descent, her hands rest lightly on the top of her thighs.

Rainwater puddled in the rut beneath her swing, which required her to clinch her knees and splay her feet to keep her feet dry. The caution, however, didn't spare the white cotton shoestring on her right Converse All-Star. On the upswing, her feet brushed the sky, and on the downswing, the shoestring stood straight, as if weightless, dancing and wiggling against the blue. As she crossed the water, the lace traced through the mud puddle, rippling the rainwater.

At two-forty-five on this afternoon, the twenty-seventh day of January, the twelfth year of the new century, twelfth year of the new millennium, the six-thou-sand-year-old sun slanted in over Madie's sixteen-year and nine-month-old left shoulder, and lit her hair from behind.

I want to know what she is thinking, feeling. What dances behind those innocent eyelids of hers? But to ask her a question would be a rude interruption of Madie's moment. A violation.

The sun warms us. The sky delights. The chain squeaks. Madie swings.

I wrote this in February 2012. We recently built a swing frame of four–by–fours that are anchored with two–hundred pounds of cement in holes that are three feet deep. Now Madie can simply run out the back door to her swing, from which she can see Pinnacle Mountain.

Eighty-four years, eight wheels

Just when you think eighty-five might be a little old for a man to celebrate his birthday with a skating party, up skates eighty-four-year-old Troy Braswell, looking twenty years younger in his brand-new black two-hundred-fifty-dollar shoe skates.

Then up skates Kitty, his wife, in her brand-new white two-hundred-fifty-dollar lace-ups. She looks like she could be twenty-one years younger than Troy, which she is.

"Daddy said it wouldn't last four months," Kitty says.

Daddy — city attorney O.D. Longstreth — made that prediction forty years ago. Kitty's father was closer in age to Troy than Troy was to Kitty.

I met up with them at Arkansas Skatium, where they were training for Troy's eighty-fifth birthday party at the Skatium.

The invitation list to Troy's party is forty-four years long — the number of years he was in the roller-rink business. They are inviting any and all who ever skated with Troy.

Troy is the king of roller rinks in central Arkansas. At the height of his reign, he owned nine — eight in Arkansas and one in Texas — with names like The Rink, The Rink 2 and Eight Wheels.

A long time before he married her, Troy taught Kitty Longstreth to skate, and he almost blew his future. When Kitty was nine-ish, which would have made Troy thirty-ish, Kitty skated up and asked Troy to play "Short Fat Fannie" on the record player.

"He said, 'You're short fat Fannie.' That made me mad. I quit skating."

Fifteen years later, however, she was in the middle of a divorce, a twenty-four-year-old mother of a five-year-old and an eighteen-month-old. She was teaching the boy to skate at the Rollerdrome on Asher Avenue, Troy's first rink. Troy, who knew her father, asked her out, but she turned him down.

"As far as I was concerned, I was still married, and I wouldn't date until I was divorced."

When Kitty was free to accept, their first date was to a Montessori School fundraising Christmas dance on December 20. They married February 1, which isn't as quick as it sounds.

"I had always known Troy. He knew the same people I knew. Daddy liked him because he had raised ... five kids by himself. I just knew that the Lord had brought him along to rescue me from a mess. He wasn't a smoker, a drinker, and he didn't run around on his wife."

Forty years later, Troy and Kitty still spark. "Soulmates," he says.

Later Kitty told me: "That's the first time I've heard him say that."

But she's good with hearing it from Troy, who avers that to stay fit he works out and golfs.

"And chases after me," throws in the mischievous Miz Kitty, her laugh as joyful as Troy's is uproarious.

~ **January 30, 2011**

Two-hundred-fifty-two years in the same building

You think you've been working a long time.

There are four people at the *Arkansas Democrat–Gazette* who have written the book on long careers with the same company.

Here's what I figured out when I wrote about them for *Between Editions*, the *Democrat–Gazette*'s in-house newsletter:

The four of them have logged a combined two-hundred-fifty-two years on the job — an average of sixty-three years.

A lot of folks retire by the age of sixty-three. These four were just warming up when they hit that age.

Some time ago, when Cecil Atwood was working at the *Hot Springs New Era* newspaper, his boss showed up with his new grandbaby. Cecil oohed and ahhed.

Twenty-seven years later, that baby, Walter E. Hussman Jr., became Cecil's boss.

Cecil, who guards the front doors of the *Arkansas Democrat–Gazette*, has worked for Mr. Hussman's family in one place or another for more than sixty years. Cecil's father was working at the Hot Springs paper when C.E. Palmer, Mr. Hussman's grandfather, bought it in 1929.

Bill Taylor officially hired on here in July 1942 at the age of fourteen. That, kids, was sixty-six years ago.

But Bill already had been throwing a paper route for a year. And on his newspaper route one day in August 1942, he made a significant discovery.

"I was walking home after finishing my route. At the corner of Fourth and High, I saw a friend from school with a very pretty girl ... ."

A few days later, Bill walked into a classroom: "There she was." And no one was sitting in the desk next to hers. Six months later, they went on their first date, and he never dated another.

Years later, after they raised their six children, his wife, Juanita, finished her college education, and John Robert Starr, managing editor of the *Democrat*, hired her as its religion editor.

Every two weeks, Jean Bradley likes to tell people, she's one of the most popular people in the building.

Jean works in payroll, a job she was doing when the company still paid employees in cash.

They counted out the bills and the coins and stuffed them into envelopes.

Jean started at the *Democrat* in 1946. "Put in there that I was seven years old," she says.

When the Hussmans bought the *Democrat* in 1974, Jean was still ciphering with a hand-cranked adding machine.

"After they came," she says, "we modernized."

Jim Wyckoff, who has worked for the *Democrat* for sixty-six years — almost twice as long as Mr. Hussman has owned it — holds this distinction: Though he retired from the circulation department and went part time in 1988, his bowling column is the longest-running locally written feature in the newspaper.

Way back when, when Jim was working in the newspaper's mailroom, he wrote about bowling, his pastime, for free.

In 1950, sports editor Jack Keady asked him to write a weekly column, to which Jim replied: "I'm not a journalist."

That, kids, was fifty-eight years ago.

~ December 14, 2008

Cecil Atwood retired in 2006 at 80. He died October 29, 2012, three months after the death of Jean, his wife of sixty-four years. He was eighty-six.

Jean Bradley retired in December 2006. She lives in Conway.

Bill Taylor retired in 2006. But he still reports in coat and tie every day to the Democrat-Gazette *building, where he runs the company's credit union from an office on the newspaper's mezzanine.*

Jim Wyckoff's last column, published December 9, 2009, included his regular column-ending report of tidbits that he called DIS 'N DATA. Jim officially retired August 12, 2010. He died October 26, 2010. He was eighty-three

Miss Tiffany Michelle Pierson didn't pick pink

Pink, Miss Pierson promptly points out, isn't her preference.

"Pink," says she, "is not my signature color."

But pink is what the company shipped.

"I wanted a white scooter," says Miss Pierson — Tiffany Michelle Pierson — "but I was too excited to send it back."

Peace with pink was the easy part — the scooter arrived in pieces.

"You can buy it three ways," Miss Pierson says: Drive it off the lot. Order it from the Internet assembled. Or order the kit — "Assemble it yourself," she says. "Save half."

Here is where we step back and have a look at Tiffany Michelle, who stands five-foot-ten, wears bright red lipstick and who named her dog Remi — for her Remington shotgun. She is, after all, from Texas.

And the pearls. Those pearls strung around her neck are real.

"I like classic things," says Miss Pierson, all of twenty-three. "My alarm goes off in the morning, and I reach for the pearls.

"It's silly to blow three-hundred dollars, four-hundred dollars on trendy. Trendy is a very expensive habit."

Miss Pierson moved to Little Rock in February to establish residency with a goal to enroll at the University of Arkansas for Medical Sciences.

Miss Pierson, whose ambition since the age of four has been medicine, graduated from the University of Oklahoma with a degree in zoology.

She chose UAMS after she met Linda DuPuy during a job fair at OU. Ms. DuPuy is director of medical-student admissions and recruitment at UAMS.

Miss Pierson liked what she learned about UAMS' philosophy of medical care, which, she believes, is personal and humane.

"Medicine is intimate," she says. "To take out the human touch . ..."

As long ago as she can recall, Miss Pierson planned a career as a cranial-facial surgeon. She even visited a cranio-facial surgical clinic in Ghana.

Little Rock, she says, has changed her ambitions. Arkansas — her move here is the best thing she ever has done — has been an awakening. She intentionally settled into a neighborhood that is nothing like the one in which she grew up near Dallas.

"I see girls walking down the street, pregnant, smoking. They're not getting medical care. Fetal alcohol syndrome is big. I know what it looks like," she says. "Cranio-facial surgery isn't what they need."

Now she thinks maybe she'll open an obstetrics clinic for pregnant teens. She wants to ensure "that children come into this world with a healthy start."

While she awaits for acceptance into medical school, Miss Pierson works three jobs — at a Starbucks, at Juanita's, and at Kaplan, a test-preparation center.

She chose to work that way so that she would see more of her new town, meet a wider variety of people.

She bought the scooter because the V-8 Jeep drinks too much gasoline.

She studied for two weeks, assembled her scooter — bled the brakes and everything — and set out on it although she never before had ridden one.   And though pink wasn't her preference, she accessorized appropriately: Pink Helmet. Pink scarf. Pink-and-green rubber boots. Pink backpack.

Only the pearls are white.

~ **November 13, 2008**

Of broken bones and bonding

Les McGregor, who was injured on the final play of the first half of the season-opening game as he leaped to catch a pass, was strapped flat in the back of the ambulance, one arm draped over his face.

The pain in his left hip was excruciating; he was sick at his stomach. In his agony, Les was only slightly aware of his surroundings as the driver backed the ambulance to pick up a second man, who also was suffering the agony of a busted hip, his right one.

The medics lashed the second injured man to a backboard, then tied him down next to seventeen-year-old Les.

Les looked at the man.

This man who had busted his hip and was now strapped in next to Les was not in uniform. The man was too old to play high school football.

Les was not hurting so badly that he didn't recognize the man immediately.

"Dad?" Les said.

Then: "You okay?"

"I'm okay," said the man with the busted hip.

"I'm hurting pretty bad," Les told his dad. "Feel like I'm going to throw up."

"Well," said his dad, who was suffering matching pain in his right hip, "throw up against the wall."

•   •   •   •   •

Until the final play of the first half of the first football game of the season, the game had been going well for Les McGregor, a six-foot-three two-hundred-pound tight end for the Cabot High School Panthers, "a dream tight end," in the words of his father.

With one minute and forty-nine seconds left in the first half, Cabot, leading twenty-seven to eight, forced the Jacksonville Red Devils to punt. Cabot returned the kick to the fifty-yard line.

He didn't know it, of course, but at that moment, Les was five plays from a ride in an ambulance and the end of his football career.

Four plays later, the refs spotted the ball on Jacksonville's forty-three-yard line.

The quarterback barked for the snap, dropped back ten yards and unleashed the football in a perfect spiraling arc toward Les, who was undefended and running full out.

As Les' right foot touched the twenty-yard line he leaped for the perfectly thrown football. A camera flashed at the moment his fingers touched the ball at arms' length above his head.

As Les pulled the ball toward earth, Red Devil No. 22, blowing out of nowhere, hurtled his direction and leaped for the pigskin too. They collided in midair, all four of their feet off the ground. Like a crash-test dummy, Les' body folded to the left in a way God never intended.

You knew Les was hurt before he thudded to the turf.

• • • • •

From the bleachers, Dale, his dad, watched the coaches' expressions as they hovered over No. 88. Dale didn't know at the moment, of course, that he was moments away from sharing an ambulance ride with his son.

Dale, who is a supervising partner of three local Sonics, walked down the bleacher steps to the rail. Coach Danny Spencer spotted Dale and beckoned him onto the field.

Students blocked his exit to the right and to the left, so Dale took the fastest route, which turned out to be the route to the emergency room: He vaulted the rail without considering that he was jumping nearly fifteen feet to the ground.

"When I hit the ground," Dale recalled months later, "I felt something snap. I went down to the right, flat of my back.

"I rolled over and got to my knees, stood up. As I put weight on the right side, it gave way, and I went down again."

So at halftime of the first football game of the 2008-2009 season, Cabot tight end Les McGregor and his father, with opposing hip injuries suffered moments apart – one self-inflicted – rode together in an ambulance.

Les, who had played a hard half of football, had suffered a simple though excruciating dislocation of his hip. His coaches had popped it back into place before Les was in the ambulance. The doctors prescribed ice and rest.

Dale, who had sat safely in the bleachers for the first half, had broken the ball off his right femur.

Early that Saturday, doctors reattached the ball. Four months later, when it wouldn't mend, doctors replaced Dale's right hip.

• • • • •

Back at Jan Crow Stadium, the Cabot Panthers put Jacksonville away 41 to 15.
~ April 19, 2009

Bekah on her feet

As soon as the Sarah Palin idea hit her, Bekah Curtis test drove it for her mother and sisters.

"In case they would say, 'That's the creepiest thing ....'"

They didn't, and the four Curtis women, formerly of Mena and now living in Chesapeake, Virginia, adopted Bekah's idea as a mission.

The Curtis women — Bekah, twenty-two, Rachel, eighteen, Elisabeth, seventeen, and mother Gena (all we'll say is she is the same age as Sarah Palin) — moved east in August 2001, leaving grandparents and other kinfolk in Arkansas.

They stayed with Gena's kid brother, Ben Fox, and his wife Tina (who now live in Mena), until, as Bekah puts it, "we got on our feet."

For Bekah, getting back on her feet means something different. When Bekah is on her feet, she is standing on her God-given left foot and her man-made right one.

Bekah was born in January 1986 with both feet, but her right foot was short one toe. The diagnosis was fibular hemimilia — her foot and leg hadn't properly developed.

When Bekah was nine months old, Dr. Richard McCarthy amputated her foot at Arkansas Children's Hospital. Two months later, Frank Snell fitted Bekah with her first prosthesis.

And twenty-something years later, the Curtis women were on their feet in Virginia, planning to attend the October 13 McCain/Palin rally in Virginia Beach. And that's when Bekah, walking on a stylish new leg, dreamed up the Palin scheme.

To personalize her newest leg, the one on which she would walk to the rally, Bekah had chosen a brown fabric printed with flowers and leaves of white. The fabric, laminated onto the leg with a clear resin, became her "skin."

• • • • •

The Curtis women left home at two-thirty a.m., stopped for protein bars and arrived at four a.m., first in line, then first inside the Virginia Beach Convention Center.

At ten a.m., the rally opened with speeches by the locals, music by Hank Williams Jr., and words from Governor Palin and John McCain.

Then Governor Palin followed McCain and his wife off the stage, and Gena's hand was the first Governor Palin shook.

The governor turned to walk the other direction, and Bekah's mission seemed to be on the verge of failure.

"Sarah," Gena called. "My daughter would like for you to sign her leg."

Governor Palin didn't respond.

Gena called again: "My daughter would like for you to sign her artificial leg."

This time the governor turned back.

"Oh, yes. okay," Governor Palin said. "I haven't been asked to do this yet."

The governor, now fully engaged, leaned toward Bekah as Bekah pulled off her leg.

"How did you lose your leg?"

"Congenital defect," Bekah said.

"Bless your heart."

The governor held the leg like a trophy. "It's beautiful," she said.

With a black Sharpie, the governor inscribed "Sarah" over one ankle and "Palin" over the other.

"I'm so honored that you let me do that." She hugged Bekah, hugged Gena, shook hands with Elisabeth and Rachel.

"You're inspiring," the governor said.

Three days later, still thrilled with the encounter, Bekah was looking to the future. "When this one wears out," she told me by telephone from Virginia, "I'll have the wackiest office decoration."

~ October 19, 2008

Try as he might, Kenneth Martin can't stop his customers from getting under his skin.

It's an occupational hazard.

In April, in fact, he had surgery after several customers, the exact identity of whom remains a mystery, got between two knuckles on his left hand.

He showed me the knot before the doctor took care of it.

He has tried wearing rubber gloves, but his line of work is so hands on, he really needs to feel what he is doing.

And it's not only his hands at risk. His customers have gotten under his skin as far up as his elbow. His feet aren't immune either. He always wears closed-toed shoes when he's working, but, once in a while, a customer works his way through one of Ken's socks.

Once a customer is under the skin of Ken, aside from the obvious discomfort, there is the danger of disease and infection.

Kenneth Martin is a barber at The Cut Off in Maumelle. The part of his customers that gets under his skin is hair, especially men's short hair.

"It's about like a needle," he says.

In all my forty-something years of sitting in barber chairs (something I did approximately twice a year from ages eighteen to twenty-two), I never once heard about this danger, but operators of local haircutting schools confirm Ken's story.

Tim Debose, a manager at Arkansas College of Barbering and Hair Design, calls them "hair splinters."

"I learned it as a student about eight years ago," he says. "I experienced one. They hurt just like a wood splinter but they are more difficult to see."

One of Mr. Debose's students' hairs wormed its way under a thumbnail, and he developed an infection that required a visit to a doctor.

"It swelled," he said. "You have all the bacteria, dirt and germs coming out of people's heads.

"You can wear gloves, but we're using our hands. It's an art. It's uncomfortable and takes away from the image of a hair stylist."

Linda Lee, who owns Lee's School of Cosmetology, has been styling hair since 1961. Sanitize, sanitize, sanitize, Linda says.

"They call hair the garbage can of the body," she says. "Everything that goes in your mouth ends up on your hair eventually. The hair is sitting there catching debris.

"It doesn't take but one time for it to happen. It could get into your blood stream and cause a staph infection."

Kenneth Martin, born in Picayune, Mississippi, and raised in New Orleans, started his barber career shining shoes in an Italian neighborhood in the Crescent City. He has been fighting hair splinters in Little Rock since the mid-1970s.

Sometimes removal is as simple as slipping the hair back out the same way it slipped in.

Other times, you call the doctor.

"I got a hair between my fingers," Kenneth said. "It left a hole where more could get in."

After the minor surgery, Kenneth was astonished at all the customers under his skin. "The doctor took out a little bottle full of hair."

~ **September 23, 2004**

Children's Hospital, Fourth Floor, Waiting

They were ordinary sandwiches, two of them, neatly wrapped by anonymous hands at a Subway shop, remarkable only because of the time they sat in the small waiting room.

Two, three days they sat there, undisturbed, a disturbing sight because of the story at which they hint: No one leaves perfectly good sandwiches without good reason.

This was a waiting room on the fourth floor at Arkansas Children's Hospital, the waiting room by the red elevators. Each of the two red elevators has one glass wall that opens onto the bright lobby so that you can watch your progress as the elevator rises and falls.

Plastic roller skates, a baseball glove and a wizard are among the artifacts of childhood and imagination that float in the air between the ground floor and the skylights.

The people who operate Children's pledge to those who enter that it is a place of "care, love and hope." And it is.

And the things you see prove why their pledge is so important: Children who ought to be swinging on a rope walk the halls, pushing their own IV pole, clear plastic tubing running from an arm.

You hear things, like the woman on the elevator (where you hear most things), who exclaimed: "My daughter woke up this morning and thought she was fifty-seven years old!"

And: "How long you been here?"

"Since April 15."

"Going home soon?"

A pause. Eyes brim.

Then: "My boy's not doing too good. It won't be long."

Wagons are everywhere, mostly red and often Radio Flyers, with a green John Deere once in a while. They are a four-wheeled alternative to wheelchairs, transportation that softens the knowledge that you are in a hospital, an alternative that allows sick kids to be kids.

You can a take a wagon on the elevator to the bottom and follow the mountain "trail," which is inlaid into the floor, to the courtyard. You can sit outside on rocks, listen to the man-made creek burble into the tiny pond, and blink against the reflected sunshine glinting off the water and the coins scattered on the bottom.

You can watch children who play as if they don't know they are at a hospital. You can enjoy the hope and optimism of those too young to know better, even with their tubes and bandages, and you absorb their hope.

Then you hear the ominous chop-chop of a medical helicopter landing on the roof, which can sound like hope or like tragedy.

And then you see a pair of neatly wrapped Subway sandwiches, left behind on a table in a waiting room that isn't much larger than a jail cell, as if a family left the room in a rush.

Did these sandwiches belong to the woman whose grandson was at Children's for brain surgery or the young father whose leather boots were so worn you could see the steel that protected his toes?

You talk to people like that, and you understand that in spite of the first-rate doctors, nurses and technicians, in spite of the hugs, the reassuring pats and smiles, in spite of the best care you can find, you understand that life isn't always happily ever after, and you pull your own child tight and pray for her and for the anonymous people who left in such a hurry.

~ **May 29, 2007**

The five-year-old sat in her parents' bookstore, the shelves stacked with the words of freethinkers, unbridled commentators, seekers of truth and knowledge, doctors Spock and Seuss and, of course, the Muppet parables.

And in that brief encounter, the youngster revealed a gap in her basic theological education: She apparently had never heard of God.

I have thought of that encounter since the Arkansas House passed a bill that would allow the state Board of Education to develop guidelines to teach the Bible in public schools as an objective, nonreligious academic subject. (The biill ultimately failed.)

The bill addresses a topic that extends beyond Arkansas, a concern among some educators, and not just the predictable right-wing suspects, that education without an academic study of the Bible is incomplete. Some call it biblical illiteracy.

"Simply put, the Bible is the most influential book ever written," David Van Biema, *Time* magazine's senior religion editor, wrote in "The Case for Teaching the Bible."

Some see the Bible as "so [pervading] Western culture," he observed, "that it's hard to call anyone educated who hasn't at least given thought to its key passages."

Mr. Van Biema wrote his essay in 2007 after he spent time in a high school classroom in which the teacher incorporated a book titled *The Bible and Its Influence*. Some folks in Arkansas have expressed an interest in considering the book for use here.

Mr. Van Biema gave the book, published by the Bible Literacy Project, high marks.

Literature and everyday conversation include many biblical allusions — a David and Goliath battle, washing your hands of a matter — the meaning of which fall flat without a basic knowledge of the Bible.

The memory of my first-hand encounter with biblical illiteracy at its most basic has stayed with me and persuades me that it is a worthy subject.

My four-year-old and I had settled on the floor in the children's section of the bookstore that day. Samantha chose a Sesame Street book, and the five-year-old whose parents owned the store joined us.

Spiritually minded, homeschooling father that I was, I always looked for ways to integrate God into all subject, even Sesame Street books.

So I posed a question: "Who made Big Bird?"

"God," Samantha said.

"Who?" asked the booksellers' daughter.

"God," I repeated. Still didn't ring a (church) bell.

So, yeah, a study of the Bible for a complete education sounds like a good idea, not to persuade the booksellers' daughter that God made Big Bird, only to ensure that when she encounters a creationist, she knows at least knows of Whom he speaks.

~ April 3, 2011

Frankie Clay, to quote the man who was about to launch Frankie's TV career, is "visually compelling."

If you have seen Frankie outside the Albert Pike Residence Hotel downtown, you would know what Steve Bowman means: Frankie is the fifty-eight-year-old with fifteen-inch legs, the one raking, sweeping, watering the grass or mowing it – the lawn mower handle hits him right about the forehead.

Frankie's smile is as wide as he is tall, His bald top is tan and freckled. "I was three-(foot)-ten," Frankie says, "and I prayed, 'Lord, let me get to four foot.'"

The Lord did him two inches better: Frankie made four-foot-two.

"I might be short," Frankie says, "but I'm loud."

Mr. Bowman, who earns his living making outdoors shows for ESPN2, has a regular role for Frankie — whom he met at Immanuel Baptist — in a new TV project.

Four years ago, neither church nor a TV job — any job, for that matter — figured into Frankie's life. As he puts it: "I ain't been back out in society but four years."

Frankie is a dwarf, the first born and only dwarf of the seven children in his family. The youngest child, also a boy, made six-foot-four.

As a child, Frankie countered ridicule with meanness. By his mid-20s, he was drinking heavily. He married, and he and his wife (five-foot-seven) had a daughter, who grew to four-foot-eleven. (Frankie and his wife split up after ten years.)

He cycled from drinking to rehab and back. He sobered up for the decade between the ages of forty and fifty.

Then: "I stayed drunk from 1996 to 2000."

Frankie's career has included wrestling, a short (pun intended) stint as the mascot for the Memphis Pros of the American Basketball Association, and twenty years with Crittenden County government.

Through what Frankie calls an act of God, he moved to Little Rock four years ago, sobered up and found friends at Immanuel.

Stan Parris, associate pastor for missions, recalls the first time he saw Frankie at church, where friends call him "Sweet-n-Low."

"When we stood up to sing," Mr. Parris says, "I kept waiting for him to stand."

Forty-five houseplants forest Frankie's living room, kitchen, bath and bedroom at the Albert Pike. "You can say this about Frankie," Frankie says of himself. "He loves the Lord and tries to serve Him. These last four years have been the best I've ever lived."

Frankie is okay with jokes about his height. At the Flying Fish, where we ate lunch one day, he ordered iced tea. "Small tea for you," the cashier said, and they both laughed.

Frankie leaned back in his Flying Fish chair, his left elbow propped on the chair next to him. His legs jutted straight out, his feet far from the floor.

"I can do just as much as the next man," he says. Pause. "But sometimes I need a stool."

And this: "Frankie's patience is like his legs."

And "Frankie's last name is Clay. When God got ready to make Frankie, he ran out of it."

Mr. Parris, Frankie's six-foot-five pastor friend, likes to tell this story: On a mission trip to Central Asia, he and Frankie bunked together at the top of an A-frame room. "For the first time in his life, Frankie actually bumped his head on the ceiling," Mr. Parris says. "It thrilled him to death."

~ October 2, 2007

A star is about to be born

A dwarf star. On the fifteenth day of October.

You've seen him around town, mostly around the Albert Pike, where he keeps the grounds.

Starting mid-October, those of you who watch television are going to see a lot more of Frankie Clay.

"We had searched all over the country, talking to companies who specialized in small people," says Leslie Dunn, executive producer at Dempsey Film Group in Little Rock. "Rob happened upon Frankie. It was almost like a Christmas miracle."

Which is appropriate since Frankie's film debut is as an elf in a commercial that promotes Breakfast with Santa, part of the Festival of Trees fundraiser for CARTI.

Rob is Rob Bell, a founder of Eric Rob & Isaac Ad Guys agency. He attends Immanuel Baptist Church, where Frankie also is a member.

Stan Parris, associate senior pastor, connected Frankie and Rob.

"He's even got his own costume," Stan told Rob.

So a week ago Monday, Frankie met the film crew at a house that overlooks the Arkansas River and spent five hours filming the public-service announcement, which required Frankie to make pancakes and a huge mess.

"He blew us away," Rob says. "It's kind of a slapstick spot. He knew exactly what to do."

Neither Rob nor anyone else associated with the project need have worried about Frankie's sensitivities about his height, which is four-foot-two.

Frankie endured meanness and ridicule as a kid and young man, but he is beyond that. Though he's capitalized on his stature in the past, he's never had an opportunity like this. At sixty-one, he is excited that his size might actually pay off.

The commercial-makers share his excitement.

"You have to be careful pulling people off the street," Leslie says. "You never know how they will be to work with ... their temperament.

"He was perfect. The expressions on his face. He was very elfish in nature. Flour was flying ... sugar, eggs. He had a great attitude, a lot of energy, a big smile."

Alison Melson, vice president of communications and marketing with Central Arkansas Radiation Therapy Institute (CARTI), has seen a version of the thirty-second commercial.

"It looks like something that was made in Hollywood," she says.

Frankie has been elfing at parties and schools for years, but his time in the kitchen was a new experience.

Never before had he griddled pancakes.

"I threw eggs, batter, stirred, sifted," he says. "I was flipping pancakes over my head."

He is taking it all in his short stride, still cutting the grass and doing the other odd jobs he picks up to make ends meet, but if the silver screen summons, he'll park the lawn mower.

"I've already had a call from another producer," Leslie says. "He's a natural. Frankie is a star."

~ October 2, 2007

• • • • •

Frankie's other small-screen credits include ads for Gwatney Chevrolet that included roles as an Olympic runner and as a leprechaun, and an incognito part in which he dressed as a badger who was a badgering car salesman. In late summer 2013, Frankie's doctors discovered he had developed cancer. As of March 2014, Frankie was taking chemotherapy.

The boys from Bryant: A Babe Ruth epic

Never mind whether these thirteen-year-olds from Bryant won or lost the biggest baseball game of their lives.

What matters is that these fourteen baseball players played it.

A week ago Saturday, after swatting their way through state and regional tournaments, the Bryant All Stars played in the Babe Ruth World Series Championship game in Jamestown, New York.

People who watched the final game described it as "epic" and "unbelievable" and "greatest ever."

"Let the record show that the epic Babe Ruth 13-year-old World Series championship game at Diethrick Park ... will be the measuring stick for any future tournament games played here," Scott Kindberg wrote in last Sunday's Jamestown Post-Journal.

The game, Mr. Kindberg reported, lasted three hours and seventeen minutes. Between them, the two teams scored twenty-five runs, made twenty-nine hits and committed eight errors. The pitchers walked sixteen batters and struck out four.

These are the young men who were Arkansas' ambassadors to the world of Babe Ruth baseball:

Zach Cambron, Evan Castleberry, Hayden Daniel, Josh Davis, Evan Ethridge, Tyler Green, Riley Hall, Blain Jackson, Tyler Nelson, Cameron Price, Daniel Richards, Trent Rivers, Tryce Schalchlin and Marcus Wilson.

Marcus was named Most Outstanding Player of the tournament. Tyler Nelson, Daniel and Zach made the all-defense team, and Hayden and Marcus made the all-tournament team.

Jimmy Parker, who grew up playing baseball in Bryant, is their manager, and Tony Ethridge is their coach.

Coaches in the Bryant league chose the fourteen all stars from six teams that played a sixteen-game season.

First they won the district championship, and then the state, having to face a persistent White Hall team three times along the way, beating the team twice.

"They gave us trouble," Mr. Parker says. "They were a good team. They would just not leave us alone."

They played the district tournament in Dumas and the regional in Del Rio, Texas, before flying to Jamestown in mid-August on Babe Ruth's dime.

On their undefeated way to the championship game, Bryant beat the team from Sikeston, Missouri. Then, finally, they played a bunch of kids from Queens, New York, for the championship.

"That game, it was real tension-packed," says Mr. Parker, who has coached for fifteen years. "We jumped out two-nothing on them. They came right back and got five runs. I've never witnessed a game like that ... those kids never gave up, never quit."

To make it to the world $eries, of course, takes more than talent. Team parents held a yard sale, and players solicited donations at Wal-Mart. The Bryant Athletic Association contributed.

"I hadn't even begun to think about how much it cost," Mr. Parker says. "It wasn't cheap, especially on the parents. I probably don't want to know."

• • • • •

A play early in the championship game seemed to bode well for the fourteen thirteen-year-old All-Stars from Bryant: After College Point had put a runner on first, Bryant's first baseman, Riley Hall, made a heroic double play. He snatched a whistling shoe-top line drive out of the air for the first out and tagged first base for the second.

And then Bryant's shot at the championship came to this:

Seventh inning, the score tied twelve-twelve. College Point loads the bases. Batter up, no outs. A single will win the game for College Point.

The batter hits a grounder straight at Tyler, who scoops it up and throws it home to catcher Josh Davis for the first out.

The next batter bounces a grounder to Tyler, who jumps high in the air, snags it with his bare hand and throws it home all in one motion for the second out.

Next batter, bases still loaded. Tyler falls behind three balls and a strike. If Tyler walks the batter, Bryant loses.

Tyler's next pitch is a strike. Strike two.

But … the College Point runner on third thinks the pitcher has walked his teammate. He leaves third base for home, thinking he is the winning run and College Point is the champion.

The boys from Bryant are alert. Josh the catcher throws to third baseman Daniel Richards. Daniel tags the College Point player in a rundown, which throws the game into extra innings.

• • • • •

Top of the eighth. Bryant's Daniel Richards is on base, poised to score. Tryce Schalchlin singles and sends Daniel home. Bryant finishes its turn at bat ahead by a single run, thirteen to twelve.

Bottom of the eighth. Tyler Nelson is pitching for Bryant. College Point has two outs and a runner on base.

College Point's own Babe Ruth, Joseph Morel, steps up to bat. Joseph Morel, the batting champion of the 2008 Babe Ruth World Series.

If Joseph hits a homer, the College Point boys from the borough of Queens will send the boys from Bryant back to Arkansas with their first and only loss of the season. And the second-place trophy.

Tyler Nelson gets ahead of Joseph: One ball, two strikes. He is one strike away from a national championship.

Tyler throws a fast ball. Joseph Morel swings like the champ that he is and drives the horsehide deep into left field.

Left field, where Marcus Wilson eyeballs the horsehide that is whistling his way. Marcus Wilson, left fielder: The difference between the championship and second place.

• • • • •

You doubt epic? Consider this: Tyler Nelson was named to the tournament's All-Defense Team. Tyler is pitching to Joseph Morel, this season's Babe Ruth batting champion. Joseph swats it to Marcus Wilson, the tournament's Most Outstanding player.

The outcome of this game comes down to the skill and nerve of three of the best young baseball players in the United States. One arm. One bat. One glove. A trinity of talent converging on a baseball field in New York for five seconds of suspense that will erupt simultaneously into glory and supreme disappointment.

• • • • •

This isn't the first time the Bryant All-Stars had been in a tight spot in this two-week tournament. In their first five games, in fact, they had to come from behind to win.

At this moment, though, the game is Bryant's to lose. They are ahead by one run.

Marcus angles left and runs back, victory or defeat riding his shoulders. He catches the ball over his left shoulder and hugs his glove to his chest.

But he loses his feet, and his momentum takes him to the ground. All eyes are on Marcus as he holds up his glove. The breath the Bryant fans exhaled was a gale-force wind that whipped the American flag straight: Marcus had hung on to the ball.

The Bryant All-Stars won the Babe Ruth World Series for thirteen-year-olds. They are the champs.

"They left everything on the field," says Jimmy Parker, their manager. "The kids kept their heads about them."

~ August 31 and September 2, 2008

Art Borel admits he asked for it.

He did, after all, plead guilty before Judge Susan Webber Wright in 1991.

Art, a native of New Iberia, Louisiana, and owner of Little Rock Auto Clock & Speedometer, fixes speedometers, a trade that has evolved from cables to electric beams during his time in the business.

Art, sixty-nine, goes so far back he already had been fixing speedometers for a couple of years by 1958, when Chrysler was the first to put cruise control on its cars — two years after it introduced under-the-dash record players.

In all those years, only once has a customer filed a complaint against Art with the Better Business Bureau. But there is the other matter.

Speedometers, dozens of them, line shelves in Art's shop. Show him a speedometer, and he can tell you what kind of car it was in.

He keeps boxes filled with tiny gears, ratio adapters and old-fashioned cruise controls that work with a vacuum.

Most speedometers are electronic nowadays, but he can still remagnetize and calibrate the old ones.

Art can clearly explain the difference between mechanical speedometers — a cable stretching from the transmission to the speedometer that turns a thousand times per mile — and electronic, which beams information from a sensor on the transy to the dashboard.

Art's customers include drivers who want him to check their speedometers because they think they have been wrongly ticketed for speeding. (About sixty percent of the speedometers are wrong, he estimates).

Among the other memorabilia boxed in his shop are "tattle-tales," devices once used on eighteen-wheelers to record their speed, miles traveled and hours of operation.

A few years ago, Art encountered human tattletales, which he was reluctant to discuss. But after a little cajoling by his wife, Janell, who was the one who brought it up, Art handed me a picture frame that had been lying flat in a bookshelf.

It was an "Executive Grant of Clemency" that President Clinton signed.

Until Clinton signed one of his infamous last-minute pardons for Art, Art had been a convicted felon.

Trouble came, Art says, during an investigation of used-car dealers, who told FBI agents that Art would roll back odometers.

The FBI wired up a few people and sent them to visit Art. Then one day, a couple of guys in suits showed up and asked if they could talk privately to him.

He admitted his crime to the FBI agents. He paid a two-thousand-dollar fine and spent three years on probation.

"I was guilty," Art says, a hint of his native Cajun accent discernible. "I didn't tell anyone about it."

His children, learned about it nearly ten years later in the February 1, 2001, *Arkansas Democrat-Gazette* in a list of Arkansans whom Clinton pardoned: Arthur David Borel, Little Rock, odometer rollback, 1991.

"You wouldn't believe the people who called," he says. "*Washington Post. CNN. Chicago Tribune.*"

Art hopes someday to thank Clinton. He can assure his presidential benefactor that his odometers are honest. "I like my freedom."

~ September 30, 2004

Foster
Mother to
furniture

Edie Barentine attracts stray furniture the way some people accumulate homeless animals.

The piece with the best history is a drafting table she bought at an estate sale in Helena in the 1970s. She no longer has it, which is what makes its story so interesting.

But all of her adopted furniture has a story, like the china cabinet with the curved-glass front that's not hers.

It came to her through her stepfather, who didn't have any children, says Edie, who grew up in Little Rock and now lives in Texarkana.

After his death, her mother contacted her husband's brother about the cabinet, which his family had carried across Kansas in a covered wagon.

"Mother told [the brother] we really wanted to get this to them," she says. "They never showed up."

She also has an oak dining table that a friend, Sue, left in her care upon her move to Hawaii. Thirty years ago.

"She had this big round oak table that had been her grandmother's. Four leaves. Banquet size. Her first request was could she store it in my attic. Before she left, she asked if I wanted to buy it. I said, no, I'll keep it for you.

"I gave her some terrible amount of money, maybe thirty-five dollars, and kept it until I moved."

Edie left contact information with a mutual friend and never heard from her again. "Everybody knows it's Sue's table."

Then there was the drafting table.

"I bought it for twenty-five dollars," Edie says. "It was a big table. Adjustable. And it was used. I love used things."

Inside a drawer she found two things: A photograph of several men, dressed in white suits and Panama hats.

And a carbon copy of a letter, written early in the last century by L.R. Parmelee, Helena's long-time city engineer and original owner of the table.

The letter was Mr. Parmelee's response to an invitation to join the Ku Klux Klan.

"He was not just declining but pretty much letting them have it," Edie says. "His words ... were very strong, very courageous. He cited the laws of God and man. He'd taken a stand ... ."

Edie, an artist who bought the table as a place to work, tucked the letter away.

Then one day at a conference in Hot Springs, Edie discerned that a woman standing next to her also was from Helena and introduced herself.

The woman responded: "You don't know me, but my father was L.R. Parmelee."

Edie recognized the name, of course, and told Janet McElduff that she owned her father's drafting table.

Janet mentioned that her son, Jim, L.R.'s grandson, was studying civil engineering.

"Well, this is your table," Edie said.

Janet and Jim came for the table. Edie refused their twenty-five dollars.

"I got a wonderful thank-you letter," Edie says.

Years later, in Texarkana, she told the story to friends. Another drawing table showed up on her carport. "No one has confessed to dropping it off," she says. "I feel like that one belongs to me."

· · · · ·

When Edie told me the story by telephone, she said that she would like to know the whereabouts of Janet and the table.

So I called the office of the mayor in Helena, where the secretary referred me to Jim Frazier, who succeeded L.R. as city engineer. Mr. Frazier, however, was out of the office. I found a phone number for his home, and his wife, Elaine, sent me to Kathryn Woods, who referred me to Laura Deitz, who sent me to her sister-in-law, Ann Faust, a former next-door neighbor of L.R.'s daughter. Fifteen minutes later, I was talking to Janet Parmelee Bondurant in Asheville, North Carolina, and she knew exactly where her father's table was.

"My son has the desk," she said. "It's up in his office."

Jim McElduff has a civil engineering firm in Asheville. At the moment, a geologist in Jim's office is using the desk. He remembers the letter Edie found, but he doesn't know where it is.

L.R. Parmelee arrived in Arkansas in the early twentieth century as head engineer on the construction of a rail line, which ended in West Helena. Eventually, he worked for the Works Progress Administration and as Helena's city engineer.

During his time with the Works Progress Administration, he oversaw construction of the city's municipal swimming pool, which is still in use.

He designed part of the city's water system, the streetcar route, which is now a city road, and the river levees.

"You can't leave Helena," Jim McElduff says, "without crossing something that [my grandfather] built."

Two carpenters who worked with L.R. built the drafting table. Jim has a 1905 photograph of his grandfather at the table, so it's at least a century old.

"It's made from two extremely wide, one-inch-thick planks. It's very plain, very utilitarian.

"It's just hammered," he says. "It's full of ... a million compass points or [holes where he was] thumb-tacking papers down so they wouldn't blow away in pre-air-conditioning days."

Jim another desk from his grandfather's office. "I'm sitting at it right now," he says during our phone chat. "It's a nice feeling, but it's a functional table. I put my feet on it. I get it dirty. I've got my coffee cup on it. Cell phone. A piece of my wife's pottery. It's got to be seventy years old if it's a day. It's solid as a brick."

~ October 7 and 10, 2004

General MacArthur's Garden Club

On a cold morning without sun, the eleven garden clubbers semicircled the newly planted, forlorn stick in MacArthur Park, eleven umbrellas angled back so eleven faces would appear in the photograph.

They stood as still as eleven statues while Lee Gershner made pictures of the MacArthur Garden Club and the six-foot tulip poplar that the city of Little Rock had planted at the club's request.

The occasion was the sixtieth anniversary of the founding of their club, named for General Douglas MacArthur, with his approval, which he gave in a letter that lies safely in a frame.

The subject of the letter, a thank-you note to a garden club from one of the world's great warriors, appears beneath the impressive letterhead: "General Headquarters, Supreme Commander For the Allied Powers."

Helen Brown brought the framed letter, wrapped in plastic grocery bags, to the ceremony. Vicki Gershner read it aloud.

"Dear Mrs. Bolton," the general wrote to Rose (Mrs. J.G.) Bolton on February 3, 1950, "I have just received your cordial note of January 10th and appreciate so much the distinction of having your Garden Club named after me. It is a rare honor, and I treasure it deeply. I have had a number of visitors in Tokyo from

Little Rock recently, and they all speak in such complimentary terms of the City. I am very proud indeed to have been born there. ..."

The women came with a shovel — its handle tied with a yellow bow — a potato rake and a garden rake, but a city employee had actually planted the tree days before.

Lois Brock, president, poked at the dirt with the shovel then planted the temporary wooden plaque on which she had spelled with stick-on mailbox letters: "MacArthur Garden Club 1949."

Then the eleven of them, plus two husbands, retreated to the MacArthur Museum of Arkansas Military History: Mary Jane Bennett, Bonnie Bradford, Mrs. Brock, Mrs. Brown, Barbara and Stan Chapman, Rosalie Deen, Jean Devie, Betty Farmer, the Gershners, Nancy Matlock and Barbara Winchell.

In the building where general-to-be MacArthur was born in 1880, they thawed and recalled the war in which his name became legend.

Mrs. Brock's memory of December 7, 1941, is as clear as yesterday. She was playing softball in a Mississippi pasture with the children of farmers who share-cropped on her family's land.

The Japanese captured her brother on Guam on December 8. For months they didn't know he had survived.

Mrs. Brown was pitching horseshoes with friends in Oden when she heard.

Betty Farmer was eating Sunday dinner with her family in Iowa when they heard the news on the radio. Within weeks, a brother and an uncle who had been sitting at the table had enlisted.

Jean Davie endured the war in her native Scotland.

"I remember the bombing of London," she says. "I remember the older people wishing the United States would hurry up. I remember the red dye they put in petrol used on farms.

"Winston Churchill came on the radio, and you didn't even breathe."

Out the window behind the storytellers, you could see the tulip poplar planted in honor of General MacArthur, starting its life in almost exactly the same place he did, a bare-limbed baby whose future was the world's. These tulip poplars, they say, can grow to a hundred feet or better.

~ March 12, 2009

At Tuskegee, he taught the ABCs of flying

Dark to dark, before and after, a.m. to p.m., Milton Crenchaw scooted round the west end of the gymnasium on spindly legs, checking the voting machines, straightening the paperwork, seeing to his poll workers.

There is a precision about chief poll judge Milton, his corners — elbows, shoulders — cut sharply, the set of his cap, the white sideburns squared perfectly at the midpoint of his ears.

The bill of his black cap juts militarily, the cap itself snugged down upon and in striking contrast to his wiry white hair.

"I run this like I ran the Army," he says.

He never actually ran the Army, of course, but he served his time, and you can imagine as you watch him scooting around that Milton took charge of whatever was at hand.

His baseball cap is a hint to his past: On the front, red stitching of an airplane and the words: "Tuskegee Airmen."

Milton didn't fly combat with the famed fliers. But at that college down in Alabama, now known as Tuskegee University, he taught them to fly, hundreds of young black pilots who went on to fly escort in World War II.

"I just taught them the ABCs of flying," he says. "Like the first grade."

His career in the air was unlikely and unexpected. Other than seeing Charles Lindbergh on his visit to Little Rock, he knew little of planes.

"I didn't even know how to spell aviation," he says.

In 1939, he left Little Rock on a bus bound for Tuskegee, where he planned to study automobile mechanics, furthering the training he received during two years at Dunbar Junior College.

But the Army needed more pilots and established a training post at the college that Booker T. Washington founded.

Milton entered the Civilian Pilot Training program, learned to fly and then trained others. Though he never flew a fighter himself, his students flew them all over the world.

The airmen desegregated the military and made history in other ways, says Milton, which was a surprise to many.

"The government hired me thinking I didn't have the sense to come out of the rain," he says and laughs.

None of this has a thing to do with his job as chief judge at the Greater Christ Temple Pentecostal Church voting site. But it is a good thing to know that a man of such accomplishment (he has a Congressional Gold Medal) and precision and the sense to flee bad weather was in charge of voting in one place in the United States.

Milton made the world feel safe.

He swore in five poll workers in one quick ceremony, and then separately he administered the oath to two latecomers. He was ready to open the doors by five past seven a.m. and might have if his poll workers hadn't pointed out the time.

Milton is happy with life, past and present.

"My job is to bring peace to the world," he says.

Milton is eighty-nine but looks seventy. At the end of his fourteen-hour day in service to democracy, Milton was as bright as he had been at seven a.m.

"Don't be looking at your watches" because that's like watching water boil, he had advised the eager folks waiting in line at seven a.m. "You'll be here all day."

They, of course, weren't, but he was, Milton Crenchaw, chief judge, scooting round, a lifelong participant in history.

~ **November 6, 2008**

These hands of Johnny Johnson's

They delivered death and life, these hands of Johnny Johnson's, and measured against the hours of his eight decades, the life-taking and life-giving were practically simultaneous.

Mr. Johnson doesn't know whether it all happened on June 6, 1944, or on D-Day and the day after, but the details remain vivid.

He was an eighteen-year-old Army medic, fresh off his family's farm in Parsons, West Virginia, that day he belly-scooched through the American bodies on the French beach near Villiers-Fossard.

Medics weren't allowed to carry weapons, but as German bullets zipped overhead, Johnson armed himself with two hand grenades from one of his fallen comrades.

This is the way Mr. Johnson, seventy-nine, told his story over a bowl of chicken-and-rice soup: "As soon as I hit the beach ... I grabbed ..." He stopped a moment then said: "It'll come to me in a minute."

Then he resumed: "... two hand grenades. I pulled the pins and threw them in two different holes. Boom-boom."

He can't say whether the next event was an hour later or five. As he walked into Villiers-Fossard, a French woman, pointing to the red cross on his sleeve, put his hand on her stomach and said: "Docteur! Bay-bee!"

"I delivered that baby right there in the road," Johnson says.

On the way out of Villiers-Fossard, another French woman approached. "This girl pulled on me. She took me into a house. There was a woman in a back room. Shrapnel had nearly torn her arm off. I got the chance to patch it up."

Soon, though, Mr. Johnson himself was in need of repair. A bullet struck him in the thigh; he tried, unsuccessfully, to remove it. Then either a hand grenade or a mortar round fell into his foxhole. A piece of shrapnel struck him between the eyes.

He remembers soldiers pulling him from beneath a dead comrade, and a nurse slapping his face. "I thought I was in heaven, and the angels had me. It was a WAC telling me, 'You're all right.'"

But he wasn't exactly. For nineteen months, he was paralyzed from the waist down.

He didn't discuss the war with his family, says his daughter Debi, who recently moved him to Little Rock. But the trauma showed itself in nightmares; her mother would awaken with Johnny's fingers around her throat.

Mr. Johnson spent his career as a tool buyer for Union-Carbide. In civilian life as in war, he told his family, he did the best he could with what he had in the circumstances in which he found himself.

He took his family camping. He was a Boy Scout leader. He was the neighborhood Mr. Fix-It. He was easily agitated, although he aged well, Debi says, and his anger waned.

His hands, however, the hands that delivered a French baby and healed toasters and tossed hand grenades into fox holes, have stiffened because of his injuries.

At lunch, he opens packs of crackers and artificial sweetener with small scissors.

To raise his tea glass to his lips, he wraps his entire hand around the glass, palm to finger tips, and hooks his thumb over the rim, the way a soldier holds a hand grenade, as if his hand is in the grip of a bad memory.

~ September 12, 2004

'You kill them, or they kill you'

Wilbur Johnson had forgotten about killing the German captain until he read the short paragraph about it in a history of his battalion.

He was young then, just twenty-one. And the captain wasn't the first person Johnson had killed, nor would he be the last.

"If he hadn't shot first ...," Johnson says. "Either you kill them, or they kill you. You're just protecting yourself."

He was a member of the 250th Field Artillery, C Battery. He arrived in France around July 1, 1944, and fought the next ten months without a break.

A few days before Thanksgiving 1944, he and three others topped a rise and surprised twenty-six or so Germans a hundred yards down a road. The captain shot at them, and Johnson aimed his M-1 and fired. The other Germans, apparently fearing the four were leading reinforcements, surrendered.

Johnson's blue eyes never rest when he's talking; they dart from mine to the sky to the sign a hundred yards away across JFK Boulevard. Johnson, eighty-one, can read the sign without glasses, and he can read his book without help, and his memory is as sharp as his vision.

The 250th deployed with about five-hundred-fifty men. The number has dwindled to fewer than seventy-five. "We lose some every year," he says.

And every time you lose a veteran, you lose a piece of the nation's history, which was the motivation for Gabe Gentry, a college student in Conway when Johnson gave him a walking tour of Washington, D.C.

"We were discussing World War II. I was intrigued by the idea that I had a primary source. I could ask what it sounded like, what it smelled like. I could have him describe it in adjectives, not text-book terms."

Upon his return to Arkansas, Gentry, now twenty-four, borrowed a camera and filmed an interview with Johnson. Four years later, he interviewed forty veterans, including Johnson, and put their stories on ten DVDs in a project titled World War II Remembered. An Oral History of Arkansas Veterans. The Arkansas Scottish Rite Freemasons, which paid for the project, has printed a thousand copies of the documentary to donate to libraries and schools throughout Arkansas.

Gentry was struck by the veterans' modesty, among other attributes.

"They would always say, 'Oh, I didn't do much ... nothing that is interesting enough for you to come all the way out here to Sherwood.' They always feel like their role was a lot smaller than it was."

Gentry spoke of a sense of his own inadequacy, that he hasn't done enough for his country. As the veterans talked, and the memory of war played out on their faces, he felt he hadn't earned his citizenship.

"If we go to the laundromat and the bank in one day, we need a nap," he says of his generation. "Not so for them."

Wilbur Johnson saw so much war and death while he was young man fighting for the United States that he had even forgotten some of it. Johnson's young friend Gentry is making sure that the rest of us don't.

· · · · ·

The compass case is black, its metal cover worn dull.

It measures three-and-a-half inches by two-and-a-half inches. You flip the round cover to see the dial.

The compass is more accurate, Wilbur Johnson says, than the electronic Radio Shack one mounted to the dash of his Toyota.

Sixty years ago to the month, Wilbur slipped the compass from the pocket of a German captain he had just killed. The German soldier fired first. Wilbur was only twenty-one then, but he well understood the concept: kill or die.

Wilbur is eighty-one and now lives in Sherwood, and though he complains of a memory chewed by time, he recalls stories from sixty years ago, stories that don't make the history books. Slice-of-war-life stories, the day-to-day moments. Stories of boredom lurching into terror.

Or boredom segueing into supper. "If it's a hog, I'm going to kill it," Wilbur's buddy said one day when he saw movement on an island. They made for the island in a leaky boat, Wilbur bailing water, his friend rowing.

The animal was a hog. They killed it and presented it to the cook, who wanted nothing of it. "Might be diseased," he said.

The soldiers appealed their case to a captain. "What?!" he sputtered.

"It's got to be government inspected," they told him.

"I can take care of that." The captain found a red-ink pen and inscribed upon the pig: "U.S. Inspected."

"Tell him to cook it," the captain ordered, "or I'm going to court-martial him."

Wilbur chuckles as he tells the story, and he ducks his head, almost shyly, and turns his face to the left.

In a barn on another day, Wilbur exchanged his rifle for a pitchfork and went in search of eggs. As he climbed a ladder, he jabbed the fork into a pile of hay, which produced a surprised and newly injured German.

Yet another day, a driver scattered straw over the snow, pitched his captain's tent and set a heater inside. The tent caught fire.

The angry captain threatened court-martial. During the night, though, a shell landed and exploded where his tent had been. "He said forget the court-martial."

Those were the moments between deaths, the deaths of enemies and friends.

"It hasn't bothered me much through the years," Wilbur says. "But here recently ..."

He ducks his head and turns to the left.

We sit in the front seat of his car, and he hands me a plastic picture album, the kind that comes free with your photographs at the film-developing counter. The cover is green and etched with the word "Memories" in gold script.

The album holds black-and-white photos of the bodies of Poles and Jews that soldiers found piled in boxcars when they liberated Dachau, the concentration camp.

The eighty-one-year-old Wilbur Johnson saw that with his own blue twenty-one-year-old eyes. He has lived a long time with these memories.

He hands me the dead German's compass from the battlefield, the antique one that still points north. He took it when he was young, when the only direction he traveled was over the next rise with no idea what lay beyond.

~ November 11 and 14, 2004

Candy bar for a vet

Ed Butkiewicz fumbled with the miniature bar of chocolate, his arthritically stiff and swollen fingers useless against the indestructible blue-and-red wrapper.

One of his friends at the nursing home where Ed lives had dropped the chocolate on the rolling table-tray in front of him.

All else forgotten save the chocolate, Mr. Butkiewicz methodically examined it, patiently turning the little bar end to end in search of a point of entry.

After a minute, he raised the chocolate to his mouth, but his stiff fingers and store-bought teeth were no match for the wrapper.

He pulled the CRUNCH bar from his mouth, looked at it, returned it to his mouth.

I watched from my perch to the left of his wheelchair and thought I should offer him a hand in opening it.

But the candy wrapper was wet, really wet, and Big-Man Me didn't want to soil his precious newspaper-hack fingers with the saliva from the mouth of a man he had only just met.

So, to my shame, I sat on my hands, as it were, and watched this eighty-eight-year-old veteran's long fight for so brief a pleasure.

Bad enough that I, whose most brave and self-sacrificing act for my country was to memorize the Pledge of Allegiance – I was too delicate to help this man who had fought World War II for my benefit to unwrap a piece of chocolate.

And to make it worse, at that moment, I saw sincerely intended words of bravado I had offered to his daughter explode into a mushroom cloud of mealy mouth.

Only hours earlier, Mr. Butkiewicz's daughter, Mary Shere had been showing me the mementos of her father's time in the U.S. Navy. His story was of particular interest because Mr. Butkiewicz had survived the attack on the United State's Pacific Fleet at Pearl Harbor.

Sixty-seven years ago today, eleven-forty-eight a.m. Little Rock time, Mr. Butkiewicz was dodging Japanese bullets and bombs.

Ms. Shere showed me letters he had written from Pearl Harbor; his dog tag with his fingerprint; his ID cards; and photographs of a lively-eyed, sailor-capped young man.

She talked of his large hands, the hands that enwrapped hers, big hands with which he farmed and wired houses.

He is a flag-loving patriot, she said, quick to acknowledge the service of others, never speaking of his own service except on nights when he hollers in his fretful sleep.

I had said to Ms. Shere that one of my chief regrets is that I never served my country in the military, or in measurable way.

Only six hours later, I — the Pledge of Allegiance memorizer who had spoken so regretfully and sincerely of my failure to serve — sat prissily by and watched as a man who survived the bombing of Pearl Harbor, who served the United States for six years, I sat and watched as he tried with hands a-tremor to remove the wrapper from a bit of chocolate.

I who would serve my Fellow Man would not even serve my fellow man.

I watched another sixty seconds, then I patted his arm. He handed me the candy, soft from the warmth of his hands and his breath, and I ever so gingerly tore back the wrapper and handed it to him.

Next morning, my shame fully registered. For my sake, a much-younger Mr. Butkiewicz had bathed in cold saltwater, had eaten the inedible, had submitted himself to the best efforts of the Japanese to kill him.

And he inadvertently gives me the chance to repay, in the smallest of ways, a chance to give an old sailor a bite of pleasure, and my immediate thought is the unpleasantness of it, and when I finally do the right thing, the next thing I do is to dash for the hand disinfectant.

~ **December 7, 2008**

Mike Vanness would have been a millionaire in Mayberry.

He could have been the son of Emmett "Mr. Fix-It" Clark, who would have been proud to watch Mike with the bum Bunn coffee maker.

The owner of the coffee machine dropped it off Monday, complaining that it was leaking. A replacement coffee maker would have cost about one-hundred-fifty dollars. To send it to Bunn for repair would have cost forty-five dollars plus postage, and she would have been without it for at least two to three weeks.

Mike, on the other hand, fixed it in ten minutes and charged her eight dollars and ninety-five cents, which included testing it. And during that ten minutes, he also diagnosed and repaired a KitchenAid blender and set up the engraving machine to etch the name "Piper" on a baby bracelet.

Vanness is a well-known name in Little Rock. Mike's grandfather, Orville, started the family business in 1936, operating out of the Snodgrass & Bracy drugstore downtown.

Orville's sons Dennis and Van, and grandson Mike, operate out of a shop at 12th and University.

They are famous for selling and fixing electric shavers and fountain pens. And now Mike stays busy fixing almost anything else you bring in.

Mike, forty-four, is a member in good standing of the throwaway generation. But if it's a small appliance, especially one built before everything was made of plastic in China, he can fix it.

He also is a member in good standing of NASA — National Appliance Service Association — which was in business before the space-age NASA.

He is, in fact, on the NASA board of directors, which is meeting in Nashville this weekend, where the theme is survival of the fix-it shop, which has been the theme for a long time. When Mike joined in the early 1990s, NASA had more than two-hundred members. Now it has fewer than a hundred.

The shop where he and his Uncle Van spend their days is disappointingly neat for a fixit shop: Boxes neatly marked, arranged and filled with thermostats, fuses, switches, and parts for coffee grinders, electric toothbrushes, blenders and juicers.

A fifty-year-old GE toaster, labeled "does not pop up," sits on a shelf at the front of the shop, one of the few things Mike couldn't fix, but not for lack of skill. He couldn't find the parts.

He sees plenty of funny things, and he doesn't always tell customers what was wrong. Mike once found a dead mouse clogging the water line in a coffee maker. "They complained the coffee didn't taste the same."

Monday is electric shaver day at Vanness for men who shave just once a week and discover before church on Sunday that their blades need replacing. "We had three waiting for us this morning," he said.

Mike didn't grow up a fan of Emmett Clark, though now Emmett is sort of Mike's patron saint. "I watch those episodes to see what he is working on," he says.

Emmett, though, tries diagnostic tricks Mike would never try: "I've seen him," Mike says, "stick a screwdriver down in a toaster."

~ August 15, 2005

Orville Vanness Story

Orville Vanness asked for a sign.

That's all he wanted. A sign with his name: "VANNESS."

And one other thing. Orville wanted something to which he could attach the sign — he wanted his own little storefront.

Orville, in fact, already had a sign of his

own. At Snodgrass & Bracy Drugstore in downtown Little Rock, where Orville launched his career at age fifteen, Orville's employer advertised Orville's pen-repair and shaver-repair shop with a sign in the store's display windows.

"But it was a small one, and I wanted a big one," Orville told Beti Gunter, an *Arkansas Gazette* writer who published her story about Orville in July 1979. "I always wanted a sign up on the street."

• • • • •

Orville had it tough from the start. "His mother died when he was nine months old," says Dennis Vanness, Orville's second-born child and first-born son. "His father farmed him out to whoever would take him."

When Orville was fifteen, older brother Roy Vanness and his wife, Mary Elizabeth "Lizzie" Crook Vanness, took him in. In 1932, when Orville was nineteen, he married Lizzie's sister Jane "Jennie" Crook. The Vanness brothers married the Crook sisters.

"Mama was beautiful. She looked just like Ingrid Bergman," says Van Vanness, Orville's younger son whose birth-certificate name really is Van and is not a name nicked off the front of the family name. Beautiful, Van says of Mama, and, like his father, gentle and kind.

"She is the only person I know," he says, "who ever took a chicken to the vet."

About the time Orville moved in with his brother and sister-in-law, he hired on with Snodgrass & Bracy Drugstore to stock shelves and to sweep up and to undertake other minor tasks suitable for a fifteen-year-old, such as compounding powerful prescription drugs into lifesaving medicine.

The drugstore, at 120 and 122 Main Street, was a round-the-clock operation. The owners so rarely locked up, as the legend goes, that they lost the keys to the doors.

To the man who worked the overnight shift fell the job of sharpening the blades for the newly invented (1928) electric shaver. Orville agreed to help the overnight man sharpen blades, which is how Orville came to be an electric-shaver man, a savvy career step toward earning his first big street-side sign.

Orville learned shavers inside out and set up a repair business on the balcony inside the store.

Mr. Snodgrass, impressed with Orville's tinkering, asked him to try his hand at the repair of fountain pens.

Thus the young man pinned his future on two technologies: a new one, for shaving, and one that, unbeknownst to him, was past its prime.

Even as Orville's pen-and-shaver sign became a fixture in the drugstore window on Main Street, Laszlo Biro, a Jewish inventor from Hungary, was in Paris in 1938 signing the fountain pen's death warrant with his newly patented writing instrument, a pen with a ball in its point.

With the advent of World War II, Orville joined the U.S. Coast Guard so as to stay closer to home than a hitch in the Army would have allowed. After four years guarding nearly every coast in the world but those of the United States, he returned to Little Rock and moved his pen-and-shaver shop into a building he shared with a jeweler and an optometrist.

He had his sign, finally, and although the sign was a shared one, it was big and hung high over the street on his storefront.

In the sixty years since, Orville's sign has followed Little Rock's trend west and suburban: 110 Main was the first, then 207 Main; 123 West Capitol Avenue, which he expanded to include 125.

After he moved to 201 West Capitol, the family opened a store in Park Plaza and bought the Remington Shave store at 407 West Seventh, so they were managing three shops at once. Their final stop downtown was at 207 West Capitol, and eventually they moved all their operations to 5801 West 12th Street, east of the intersection with University.

Three years ago, Orville and the boys moved the business — which for more than twenty years has included grandson Mike Vanness — to west Little Rock proper, in a strip shopping center at Rodney Parham Road and Market Street, across Market from Franke's cafeteria. (Mark Vanness, Mike's older brother, worked in the shop for a decade before he joined the Little Rock Police Department. Van's daughters Gini and Juli served their time in the store, as have Mike's daughters and Orville's great-granddaughters Lyndsey and Alyx. Dennis' wife, Becky, founded the Vanness' wedding supply and gifts franchise.)

On the matter of signs and modern life generally, Dennis Vanness prefers the old ways.

"Used to," Dennis once said, "the first thing you did when you hung up your sign, you put the family name on it. Anymore, it's the 'Something Else' or the 'Fly-by-Night.'"

Orville's ticker first betrayed him in 1959, when he was forty-six. After several weeks in the hospital, he cut his two packs of Winstons a day to no cigarettes and took up gum. He rarely was without a chaw of Dentyne, which improved his health but enriched his dentist to the tune of a couple of sets of dentures, so much did he chew.

The doctors also told him to improve his diet and to slow down.

"He took his rests religiously," Dennis says.

There was a moment some years after the first heart attack that Orville's ticker signaled the possibility of another. Since the pain wasn't excruciating, Orville opted to travel by personal conveyance rather than by ambulance.

An observant customer, sensing the impending loss of opportunity, made a request of Orville: Would Orville, the customer asked, fix his shaver before he went to have his heart attack?

Orville fixed the shaver.

At the hospital, the doctors told Orville the chest pain was a false alarm.

• • • • •

Danny Fudge, a preacher in Russellville who buys, sells and fixes fountain pens, once recounted the story of a man whose fountain pen was almost beyond fixing.

"You're looking at fifty dollars to repair this pen," he told the man. "This pen isn't worth fifty dollars."

"It was my mother's pen," the man said.

"Say no more," Danny replied.

"He [was] going to put ink in that pen and write with it, the pen his mother wrote with. It's a connection to the past."

$$\bullet \quad \bullet \quad \bullet \quad \bullet \quad \bullet$$

Orville Isaiah Vanness is a connection to the past. Born early in the century past, he lived a decade into the new one.

Orville started his career sharpening blades. In his latter years, Orville made an art of dulling them.

There was no rock or limb on his six acres that Orville wouldn't challenge with his Kubota tractor or his John Deere. "Van had to buy blades every time he turned around," Dennis says.

Orville Vanness was born on January 30, 1913, and died March 20, 2010.

Orville was preceded in death by Jennie Crook Vanness, who died in 2003, and by their daughter, Beverly Ann, who died in the middle of the Great Depression at the age of three, and by a grandson, Joey, who didn't see twenty-five.

On March 29, Orville's family and friends ferried him from the Landmark Missionary Baptist Church across the parking lot to the cemetery, where they set the coffin over his final stop.

"We've gone as far with Orville as we can," the preacher said.

Days after the funeral, Van and Dennis were telling stories about their father, such as the one about the doctor's prediction after Orville's first heart attack that he would live to a hundred.

"How do you know that?" Orville asked.

"Because you'll take care of yourself."

The doctor missed his prediction by three years. Orville made ninety-seven.

$$\bullet \quad \bullet \quad \bullet \quad \bullet \quad \bullet$$

Orville Vanness was thirty-three when he hung out his shingle in 1946.

In the sixty-four years since, a year has not passed that there hasn't been a Vanness sign over the front door of at least one store in Little Rock.

If you travel far enough south from Little Rock on Arkansas 367, and if you look east before you arrive in Landmark proper, you will see another of Orville's signs — a street sign that marks Vanness Road, which is the official access to their six acres.

There's one more Vanness sign of sorts, a much newer one, a little farther south. By sundown on March 29, the mortal remains of Orville Isaiah Vanness lay there, he facing east, this other sign above and behind his head, his name carved in stone.

~ April 25, 2010

The Vanness family now sells fountain pens and wedding supplies from its shop at 11610 Pleasant Ridge Road in the Pleasant Ridge Shopping Center in Little Rock.

stumped

"Crushed like an accordion" is the way Troy Crenshaw describes what happened to his left leg upon his sudden stop at the bottom of a tree he had climbed. So badly crushed that his doctors had to trim his leg off below the knee.

Reckon what ol' Troy did after that?

He crashed his motorcycle on I-630 and so royally busted up his right leg that he now has a pair of matching residual limbs, by which we mean twin stumps.

"My grandmother always said, 'Someday, you'll wish you'd listened,'" Troy said the other day as we sat in the shade of the narrow porch on the front of the house where he lives in Levy.

Wasn't only his grandmother who warned him. All his life, says Troy, God has put smart and good people in his life to wave him off his self-destruction. Most of the time, he has ignored the advice.

He acknowledges that most of his scars are self-inflicted: He had no idea, for instance, that the fellow in the bar in Texas would shoot him in the back, but he most certainly knew he was inviting bodily harm when he flirted with the man's girlfriend.

Scrapes with death are routine, and he has had his brushes with the law, like the night in January 2005 that Little Rock Police arrested him because he asked another man for a cigarette. At the point of a knife.

Some of the self-infliction is inherited, avers Troy, who grew up in New Mexico in a family that he says traces moonshiners back nine generations. When he was a crying baby, his mother muzzled him with moonshine from a baby bottle.

This shy of fifty, he doesn't complain. He is intent, rather, on outrunning his blunders even if he must run on legs that look like aluminum broom handles. He has bought and reassembled an old junker with a trunk just big enough to hold his push lawnmower.

"He's probably the most — can I say stubborn? — and determined person I've ever met," says Steve Street of Hanger Prosthetics & Orthotics, who customizes and assembles Troy's high-tech prostheses from the top of the socket pocket that attaches to his residual limbs — the stumps — to the soles of his bionic feet.

Troy is unusual in Steve's experience in another regard: He lost each leg independent of the other.

"It's not very common to lose limbs in separate incidents," Steve says. "For two traumatic accidents that are individual accidents, that's petty rare."

Troy is hard to miss as he pushes a mower across a lawn on his legs of aluminum, which is what he was doing when I noticed him at Maumelle Boulevard and Counts Massie Road. He's the only legless lawncutter I've ever met.

He can build a house, he says, and wire it. He worked in the oil patch. He can fix cars, and tow them, but he believes this lawn service will put him on his feet. He's fully aware that his track record ain't so hot. But right now he is sober and drug-free, he says, and working when he can find it: "I'm going to see what I can do now to finish the race right."

~ April 21, 2011

Making music, if not friends, with M&Ms

For those who are Emily-Post challenged, here are some of the Miss Manners sorts of things I have learned, mostly the hard way, about proper behavior at events of culture now that my two violinist daughters are in the Arkansas Symphony Youth Orchestra.

These rules of etiquette are a matter of urgency for those of you who plan to attend (and you oughta) the Side-by-Side concert, in which the members of the upper-level youth orchestra play alongside the professional musicians of the Arkansas Symphony Orchestra.

Ignore this wisdom at peril of great embarrassment, assuming you still have the capacity for embarrassment. If necessary, clip and slip this column into your shirt pocket, or, if your T-shirt doesn't have a pocket, into the top of a sock (yes, you should wear socks).

For starters, the authorities generally discourage tailgate parties around Robinson Hall. Downtown Little Rock really isn't set up for it.

Inside the concert hall, best leave off your Valvoline hat, even if it matches your T-shirt. The smell of Whole Hog barbecue tends to distract. So unless you take enough sandwiches for everybody, those are best left in the pickup. Beverage tip: There is no convenient place in the concert hall to set your Big Gulp, at least those bigger than sixty ounces.

The musicians — even the younguns — don't appreciate attempts to throw M&Ms into the sound holes of their violins, violas, stand-up basses, et cetera.

If you insist on sharing your candy, however, the horns, especially the tubas, are an easy target. Word to the wise: Peanut M&Ms have a better heft for throwing from the cheap seats, which is where you undoubtedly will end up, if you are inclined toward such sport.

Head bobbing and neck jerking along with the music is okay, although the more sophisticated occasional nod of your is preferred. Never stand in your seat. Until, that is, you have checked behind you to ensure you won't block someone's view. Dancing is never okay, even to the Lone Ranger Theme.

And this advice is the most often ignored, so write it in the palm of each hand with a black Sharpie: Never, under any circumstance, be the first person in the audience to clap when a song is over. Just because the orchestra quits playing, doesn't meant the song is over.

The youth orchestra program has three levels: Preparatory, John Jarboe conducting; Academy, Tom McDonald conducting; and Youth, led by the Julliard-trained James Hatch, principal bassist for the ASO who has conducted the youth orchestra since 1983.

The youth orchestras draw two-hundred young musicians from thirty-seven communities as far away as Fort Smith, Batesville and Quitman, says Barbara Burroughs, manager of the youth orchestras.

Andrew Russell, eleven, is concertmaster for Prep, and Abby Harkins, ten, is assistant concertmaster. Stan Ma, thirteen, is the Academy's concertmaster. Samantha Grelen, sixteen, (yes we are, I'm proud to say, related) and Philip Baca, eighteen, are co-concertmasters for the Youth level; Catherine Thompson, seventeen, is assistant concertmaster.

The concertmaster, for those who don't know a kettle drum from a tea kettle, is the conductor's right-hand musician, although the concertmaster sits to his left. The concertmaster walks onstage ahead of the conductor and tunes the orchestra. At the end of the concert, the conductor usually shakes the concertmaster's hand in appreciation for protection from pieces of flying candy.

If you do go, by the way, add this to your list of cautions: As the last strains of Beethoven fade into the acoustically engineered rafters, this is neither the time nor the place to hold your cigarette lighter over your head and scream "Free Bird."

~ January 26, 2006

For you Arkansans who seek significance wherever you find it, here's a fact to tell the grandkids: Hootiepuckers — the word not the attitude — apparently originated in right here in Arkansas, possibly near West Memphis.

I learned the word from the Mountain View Taylors, the family that owns the Laid Back Pickin' music barn.

"I don't know where it came from," says Barbara Taylor, who thinks she learned it from Grandma Craig, a family friend who owned a country store near West Memphis. "I thought everybody says it."

The hootiepuckers fall somewhere between mildly disappointed and angry. It's one emotion shy of "bent out of shape."

"Like kids, when they don't get what they want," John Taylor says. "They're not squawling and bawling. They're pouting, all puckered up."

Teenagers and musicians are especially susceptible to the hootiepuckers.

"I always thought it belonged to us Crutchfields!" exclaims Sarah Crutchfield Goodman, who lives near Prattsville — which is, to use her words, "a booming metropolis with a reported population of three-hundred-thirty." Her family has long used the term, although with a slightly different meaning than the Taylors'.

"Technically," she says, "I've never lived in Prattsville. I grew up outside the city limits in a community called Dogwood. I like to say I lived in the 'suburbs' of P-ville. When I married, I moved a whole eight miles away. Now I live outside the city limits on the other end of town in a community called Sweet Home. It's next to places with colorful names like Tight Wad and Dirty Ankle."

Anyway, on the matter of the hootiepuckers, she writes: "When a child cries until he can't get anything out except a few pitiful, gasping sobs, that child is said to have a case of the hootiepuckers. My mother calls the same soundless, heaving crying 'snubbing.' I have a fairly dramatic three-year-old son, so I get to use this word quite a bit. I assumed hootiepuckers was my sister's own personal invention because she's the first person I ever heard say it."

Joyce Howard of Batesville offers a definition quite different.

"I first heard the term in the late 1960s at Swifton," she wrote, "and it referred to chill bumps. ... It is a fun term to use with children. ... They usually give me a funny look and then smile and ask, 'What's that?' ... I like [my definition] best and will continue to use it whenever there is a chill in the air."

~ **March 5 and 16, 2006**

The curse of the high school English teacher

The question I hear most often — other than "Are your feet really size fourteen?" — is: "How do you find enough stuff to write about?" My answer: "The question is not how do I find enough stories to tell, but how do I find enough time to tell all the stories I find?" The four columns that follow illustrate the point. Vicki Morgan, a friend who is a long-time employee of the Democrat-Gazette, *tells many stories about her fearless father's career as a Little Rock police officer. One of her stories involved a rookie cop who went on to become a well-known law-enforcement guy in Pulaski County. When I interviewed that officer for the column about his experience with Vicki's dad, the next obvious column was a story about his interesting name, which led to a column about how his mother and wife felt about his nickname and about the cop who tagged him with the nickname, which led to a fourth column about a state police officer who risks his life to road-test inexperienced and unlicensed drivers. See? Easy. Stories fall from the sky.*

Second day on the job, fresh out of the academy, Little Rock cop Charlie Holladay is riding in a patrol car with Will Morgan, a seasoned cop.

Second day of his career, Charlie and Will rush to a store where the owner has shot a gun-toting man who tried to stick him up.

Second day: The storekeeper fills in the details for the rookie and the veteran, who are standing in front of the brick building, which once was a Little Rock fire station.

Forty years later, this is how Charlie, no longer a rookie, recalls that moment: "We knew he had a gun. We knew he was still in there. We were fairly sure that he had been shot. We didn't know if he was still alive."

Those were the even riskier days for police officers, the days before portable radios and SWAT teams whose members trained for such danger.

So it's the two of them, a seasoned forty-two-year-old veteran twice the age of his unseasoned twenty-one-year-old partner.

The veteran hollers: Come out, or we're going to have to come get you.

Then the veteran says to the rookie: We're gonna have to go get him.

"I'm fresh out of rookie school," Charlie recalls. "My heart's pumping a hundred miles an hour."

Charlie Holladay, who now has been in law enforcement for as many years as Will Morgan had been alive that day, has only admiration for the officer who walked him through his baptism of fire, which easily might have been a baptism of gunfire.

Charlie — better known now as Pulaski County Sheriff Doc Holladay — says of Will Morgan: "Fearless. Will was a fearless guy. Rock solid. Strong as a bull. Shaking your hand, he [would] make it ache. He didn't back up from anything."

He and Will shared other adventures. "We got a couple of ... domestic cases. And we had a scuffle or two, people we'd have to arrest. But that particular incident has always stood out in my mind. My first time riding with him ... to have that happen and see how he responded. Our friendship grew after that.

"Will was a good teacher, patient, but he could be pretty clear when he told you what he wanted. When it comes to writing a report, he'd check my work ..."

Will, who retired in August 1987, lives in the Greenbrier earthquake belt with Colleen, his wife of fifty-eight years.

"He's still stout," says the sheriff, who mostly sees Mr. Morgan at funerals and an annual fish fry. "He could still handle himself if he had to."

On his second day as a cop, the rookie destined to become sheriff treads cautiously into the store.

Guns up, Will goes right, and Doc left, which is the direction of the counter and the cash register.

"We're slowly moving around," Doc says. "I looked over the counter, and there was this kid lying on the floor with a gunshot wound in his left leg, a gun in his hand.

"I yelled at him to drop the gun. He was hurt. He was ready to give up."

~ April 14, 2011

What else would you call him?

Even the sheriff's mama and his wife have surrendered and refer to him as "Doc" when they're talking to folks outside the family.

That's not his real name, of course, nor is it either woman's preference. But if they called Doc Holladay by his birth name, nobody would know they were talking about the sheriff..

A 2005 story in the *Arkansas Democrat-Gazette* identified him by his given name and referred to him as "a retired Little Rock police captain." Upon reading that, most Little Rock police officers, retired or otherwise, likely said: "Who?"

"Everybody in the department knew who Doc Holladay was," Doc says. "There weren't a dozen who knew my real name."

Although his real name appears on his driver's license and all his official personal documents, everywhere in his professional life he is "Doc."

"Doc" appeared on the ballot both times he has run for sheriff, and he uses "Doc" on his business cards, his sheriff's department letterhead and his signature stamp.

John Gravett, a retired Little Rock police officer, claims credit for tagging him with the nickname two days after Doc started, says Doc, who was twenty-one when he first rode with Mr. Gravett. "It just sort of hung on throughout my career. I like it. It's served me well."

For the sheriff, who has worked in law enforcement his entire career, the name is perfect. The original Shootout-at-the-OK-Corral Doc was a dentist who turned gambler and gunslinger, occasionally in pursuit of law and order. (The original Doc's last name was double "L" then an "I;" our Doc is a double "l" then an "A.")

"The truth is," Doc says, "if your name is 'Holladay,' and you're a male, and you're in the workplace, the likelihood of becoming a 'Doc' is not uncommon at all."

Doc's brother Larry, who wasn't in law enforcement, and their late cousin, Tommy, who was in the sheet-metal business, both were Doc Holladays.

Doc, the one who is sheriff, has thought of changing his name in the records, but never seriously. "Out of respect for my mother," he says. His parents took his first and middle names from uncles.

"I'm okay with it," says his mother Martha. "I call him Doc sometimes."

Hiw mother and Debbie Holladay, the woman who married Doc forty-one years ago, acquiesced to the nickname after he entered politics. Doc and Debbie have two sons, neither of whom have picked up the nickname for themselves.

So, Doc, what is your real name?

"Well, uh," he says as if he has to recall it. "Charles."

~ June 14, 2011

His name or her vote

It was only one vote, but it was an important vote to Doc Holladay in his first run to become sheriff of Pulaski County.

He had to choose — would he put "Doc" on the ballot and risk losing that vote? Or would he go with his given name, Charles, and sacrifice the name recognition he had built in Pulaski County?

For Linda Napper, a North Little Rock marketing and campaign expert, there was no choice.

"During the first [campaign] he told me he was not sure if his mother was going to vote for him if he used the name 'Doc' on the ballot," Linda wrote to me after she read the Sweet Tea column about Sheriff Holladay's nickname. "I explained that we might just have to risk losing her vote to get everyone else's."

Well, Doc ran as Doc, twice, and his mother's disapproval notwithstanding, he won both of his campaigns, which attracted national attention.

"We ... received several requests from all over the country for his yard signs," Linda reports. "Usually they would ask if we really had a man named Doc Holladay running for sheriff. I would say, 'Yes,' but explain the difference in the spelling.

"That didn't seem to matter. Most who called were political junkies or Western fans. There is no telling where all the signs are displayed."

~ **June 21, 2011**

Cars plum full of empty Coke cans

In his first career, John Gravett wore a badge on his chest and a sidearm at his waist.

He knew the next speeder he stopped might stick a loaded pistol in his belly, or that at the next spouse-house fight, he might be the one to leave with a cracked skull.

So with that experience under his gun belt, John retired from the Little Rock Police Department in 1985 to work at a truly dangerous occupation: He tested rookie drivers who were applying for an Arkansas driver's license.

He can't tell you the number of wrecks he survived in sixteen years with the Arkansas State Police.

A dozen? He laughed: "Probably more than that."

Gravett is a familiar name in local law enforcement. His son, Johnny, is a former Little Rock officer who works in the state Crime Laboratory. His brother, Carroll, was sheriff of Pulaski County; one of Carroll's sons is a police officer, the other works in security for the Department of Veterans Affairs.

Mr. Gravett was one of the first policemen to work with a young Charles Holladay, who forty years later is in his second term as Sheriff Doc Holladay.

The intellectual jump from police sergeant to driver tester was simple: "I was already familiar with the rules and regulations of the road."

The real test was the one of his nerves. With each driver's test, he inspected the car to be used: brakes, lights, horn, et cetera.

"One day a guy come in, his car had been wrecked — the passenger door wouldn't open. He wanted me to get in on the driver's side and slide across. I told him, 'No way. I'm not getting trapped in there.'"

The back seat in another driver's car "was plum full of empty Coke cans ... up to the top of the front seat. I didn't go with him either. The rule said they had to have the car halfway decent."

He tested drivers in Mercedes, Beemers, Cadillacs and the occasional old Rambler. The most common mistake: "Driving too slow because I was in there."

Some rookies were more rookie than others: Some "couldn't even back out of the parking place."

And then there were the mishaps, like the one in which a rookie driver had stopped to turn left.

"I could hear the brakes behind us. I knew they were going to hit us. They … knocked us around. The boy already had his wheels cut [to turn], which you shouldn't do. That could have been a bad wreck."

Another day, Mr. Gravett had parked his personal car and was about to go into the office when a girl at the wheel hit his car.

The worst, though: "That day the boy hit the state police car."

"The officer had his car parked long ways," Mr. Gravett recalls. "When we were parking, the boy pulled in, and instead of hitting his brake, he hit the gas."

The impact was impressive, Mr. Gravett says.

When they had quit bouncing, the boy looked at Mr. Gravett and inquired: "Did I pass?

~ June 16, 2011

Charles did all right

Charles Deville's pals from high school would have been amazed to see him at the podium in Little Rock on Wednesday.

I can say this about Charles' high school buddies because I was one of them, roaming the halls in the early 1970s at "dear" old Pineville High School, smack in the middle of Louisiana.

Now Charles lives in central Arkansas, two-hundred-fifty miles north of where we "grew up." And in one of life's serendipitous coincidences (not all coincidences are, you know) we work at desks that are, as a pterodactyl flies, only half a mile and a river crossing apart.

Charles and his wife, Mary, moved to North Little Rock in 1997 when he accepted the position as executive director of Family Service Agency, a nonprofit that provides, among other things, counseling for nonviolent shoplifters and for those who abuse alcohol, drugs and/or people. FSA does much of its work in cooperation with city and district courts.

Charlie was one of the Catholic boys who appeared out of nowhere at Pineville High — they had spent their early years of training at Sacred Heart's schools, which stopped after the eighth grade.

Charles was popular in school, a good student, who earned a master's degree in social work.

Charlie, as was I, was one of the children of the '70s, the kids whom the adults feared, and rightly so, might not make it out alive.

Which is why the sight of Charles presiding over his agency's annual December luncheon was amazing. Charles Deville grew up to oversee an agency with an annual budget of nearly three million dollars.

And there he stood on Wednesday, his well-trimmed hair turned prematurely but handsomely white, in a sport coat and tie, addressing a group that included

Pulaski County Sheriff Doc Holladay, who is the incoming president of Charles' board.

Here's the former kid from my hometown, who easily might have traveled the wrong direction in life, now an adult who helps others who actually did take the wrong path. Adults such as the FSA client who spoke after Charles had wrapped up the business part of his program.

This woman told of riding the cocaine train to ruin and then serving nearly three years in the state pen for killing another woman with a two-by-four to the head.

Upon the woman's release from prison four years ago, Malta Willits, a counselor on Charles' staff, stepped into the life of this woman, who thanked God and Family Service Agency for her deliverance. She promised us, in the poem she wrote for the occasion, that the rose will bloom again.

When she finished reading, she tossed silk rose petals, which fell to the floor and lay at her feet, and we stood and applauded. Charles stood beside her, and my applause was as much for Charles as for the woman, whose success is one of the fruits of his.

~ December 2, 2010

Vicki Guthrie climbed the steps to her sister's apartment on a Saturday fourteen years ago, unaware these steps were still warm with the tread of a killer.

Treva Parks didn't answer Vicki's knock, so Vicki went home.

The next day, after Treva still hadn't answered her telephone calls, Vicki returned and this time, using the key with which Treva had entrusted her, Vicki found her sister dead on her bed, a gaping wound to her chest, her face slashed.

Fourteen years later, Little Rock homicide detectives' best guess was that the person who murdered Treva was a man because the blood they found on a towel in her apartment tested as male.

The wreckage in her apartment testified that Treva, a painter and a seamstress, clearly had fought hard: Furniture was overturned and shards of glass were strewn from the living room, through the dining room, and past her easel and sewing machine. The assault ended in her only bedroom.

After police finished in the apartment, Vicki was left with the cleanup. Upon stripping the bed, she saw that her sister's blood had soaked through the mattress and box spring and onto the carpet below.

That was 1990. I learned of Treva's death from the clipping my mother sent to me in Lexington, Kentucky, from our hometown newspaper, *The Alexandria Daily Town Talk*, in Louisiana. Treva had been a year ahead of me at Pineville High.

Thirteen years later, when I arrived to work for the *Arkansas Democrat-Gazette*, Treva's unsolved murder was high on my list of stories to tell.

"She had been here two weeks before for Father's Day and my birthday," Nell Parks said in an interview in their home in Pineville, the house where Treva grew up. "I felt like God had given us that time. It's been a bad fourteen years. I started a diary. I called it, 'My Life Without Treva.' It got to be too hard to write."

On that last visit, Treva dreamed that someone was chasing her with a knife, and she ran to her parents' bedroom.

Treva likely knew her killer. Police think she willingly opened the door. The face slashing could be a clue. That's a personal attack often motivated by jealousy or possessiveness.

"I think she was brutally ambushed right at the door," says Sgt. Allen Quattlebaum, chief of the Little Rock Police Department's homicide unit. "I don't know why this one is so difficult. We had a lot of people to talk to, plenty of physical evidence. It just isn't the right physical evidence."

This is one of Vicki Parks Guthrie's favorite photos of her sister, Treva, who is holding Vicki's daughter, Alison. This picture was taken in the spring before John Yancey murdered Treva.

Fourteen years later, the only "person of interest" is a man who surrendered to Little Rock police wanting to confess to a Texas murder. The case is similar to Treva's, and police say the man was in Little Rock in 1990. Texas police have not yet added the man's DNA to the national criminal database.

The person who killed Treva — if he is still alive — hasn't been called to account for her murder.

So maybe this reminder will jog a memory or jar a conscience, in the unlikely event that her killer or his friends have developed one.

There is a peephole, now, in the new door at Treva's old apartment. Window and door stickers from different security companies promise twenty-four-hour protection. The fourteen pine steps to the apartment are worn and faded gray.

~ August 29, 2004

Long time coming
In the January 24, 2010, Democrat-Gazette, C.S. Murphy reported that a DNA match had led Little Rock police to a suspect in the 1990 murder. In July 2010, prosecutors charged John B. Yancey Jr. with capital murder in Treva's death. Yancey, who had served time for burglary and theft, was in jail again at the time police focused on him. Mr. Yancey, by then forty-two years old, eventually pleaded no-contest to a charge of first-degree murder. On March 28, 2012, Circuit Judge Barry Sims sentenced him to forty-five years, Democrat-Gazette court reporter John Lynch wrote. In exchange for the plea, Mr. Lynch reported, prosecutors reduced the charge from capital murder, dropped a rape charge and recommended the prison term. Under the provisions in effect at the time of the killing, Yancey can qualify for parole after serving fifteen years, only a third of his sentence.

Vicki Parks Guthrie wrote this follow-up for Sweet Tea Times at my request..

There would be no miracle that weekend. My sister didn't answer my telephone calls or my knock at her door. She hadn't called the shop Saturday morning to check on her car. No one else in our family had heard from her.

No miracle. Sometimes I wondered, is there even such a thing?

The one-year anniversaries passed: Treva's birthday. The day she died. The day I found her body. The memorial service in Little Rock. The drive to Louisiana as we followed the hearse that carried her casket (*her casket?!?*). The burial and graveside service on July 4, 1990. *Her burial?!?* Hadn't I just seen her Friday, only hours before she was killed!? Then the second-year anniversaries passed. And then the third. It didn't seem possible that I could have lived through twenty years of insanely painful anniversaries, and investigators still had not found the person who had murdered my sister.

From the details that we knew, I had created a video that had played in my head for twenty years – the last minutes of Treva's life: How hard she fought. What she might have been thinking. Whether she knew that she was going to die. Whether she called out my name for help or asked God to deliver her. Early in the investigation, we learned that Treva had left us a message, a clue, a towel stained with a mixture of her blood and a man's blood. She had managed to fight back long enough to draw blood from her attacker.

John Yancey was arrested in July 2010 for capital murder for the incomprehensibly brutal killing of Treva after his blood, entered into a national database after his conviction for another violent crime, matched the DNA in Treva's towel. Now I had a face to put with that villain.

Prosecuting attorney John Johnson doggedly fought for justice for Treva. In the end, however, it played out in a rather anticlimactic court appearance on March 28, 2012. John Yancey agreed to a plea and was sentenced to forty years in prison. Was it enough? Would anything be enough? The only real justice would be for him to die the way Treva did.

And yet in the years after this unspeakable tragedy, there were miracles. My son, Drew, was two years old and my daughter, Alison, was an infant of four months when Treva was killed. I knew at once that I would have another daughter so that she and Alison could experience the remarkable relationship that only sisters share. Alison inherited Treva's artistic abilities, and Elise, born in April 1993, inherited her natural instinct for fashion. Both of my girls have Treva's sparkling wit and share a special connection with her that transcends the impossible.

Early in 2009, Alison began a quiet quest to learn more about the aunt who had held her as in infant. In January 2010, just after police had received the hit on Yancey's DNA but before they had told us or the press, Alison visited the Little Rock Police Department. She spoke with Detective J.C. White, who seemed taken aback by her questions. Her eyes were drawn to the thick file on his desk. It was Treva's file. What are the chances that twenty years after the crime, with no evident progress in solving it, the victim's niece would visit a homicide detective and see her aunt's file on his desk just as police were tracking a fresh and promising lead?

Another miracle was reserved for my brother, Bill, who had a dead cystic kidney removed when he was six. In 1998, Bill's remaining kidney began to fail, and he was placed on the transplant waiting list. Within months his kidney failed entirely, and he began daily peritoneal dialysis. A month after Yancey's conviction, my mind cleared. I sensed a voice and a call I felt compelled to answer. I knew that neither Treva nor I could allow our mom to lose another child.

Our blood types didn't match, but I was approved as a living donor for my brother.   Five months after our information was entered into the National Kidney Registry, we had a match.

The surgery to remove my left kidney began at five-thirty a.m. while Bill's donor was having surgery at the same time in New Jersey. Our kidneys were placed in coolers aboard commercial flights, passing in the air somewhere between Houston and New Jersey. (I'd like to reserve a seat for a kidney, please.)

At ten p.m., I awoke to learn that Bill was just out of surgery and his new kidney was already working.

Bill got his life back on Tuesday, October 23, 2012, six months after Yancey's conviction. And somewhere in New Jersey, members of a family celebrated as their loved one awakened with my kidney. I never thought I'd be able to say, I have a kidney that lives in New Jersey, any more than I ever thought I would believe in miracles.

Daisey at Mile Marker 9

NEWPORT — Stacey Smith, the prison chaplain, didn't exactly steal Daisey Ellen Riley's identity.

And Stacey Smith, to be exact, wasn't exactly a prison chaplain that day she rented an RV with Daisey Ellen's driver's license and hauled eleven pounds of cocaine to Arkansas.

Stacey wasn't stealing Daisey Ellen's identity, only borrowing it long enough to rent the recreational vehicle. She never even met the real Daisey Ellen.

This was to be the first visit to Arkansas for Stacey and her two cocaine compadres, which is why the trio opted to travel in style.

"We were going to make a vacation out of it," she says and smiles at the absurdity, "in an RV loaded with cocaine."

I learned of Stacey in a story that *Democrat–Gazette* reporter Charlie Frago wrote in April. The punch line is that Stacey, released from prison in 2004, is now an assistant chaplain at the McPherson Unit, ministering to inmates with whom she served time, including a former cellmate who murdered her husband.

I wanted to hear more, so when I was at McPherson recently, Stacey took time out to share the story of her life as Daisey Ellen Riley.

The smugglers-three traveled from Texas through Oklahoma, then drove east on Interstate 40. At Mile Marker 9 inside Arkansas, state troopers blue-lighted the cocaine buggy with Texas tags.

The arrest, Stacey says, was God's answer — though not the one she had envisioned — to her plea for an escape from her life of drugs and motorcycle gangs.

She was twenty-nine, daughter of parents who were moderately well-connected in Texas politics. Stacey had worked as a page in the Texas House of Representatives.

But: There was Stacey's older boyfriend, and, when she was sixteen, the first of her five abortions. By Mile Marker 9 in 1993, she was a meth- and cocaine-wracked drug addict, riding with a motorcycle gang, selling drugs to pay for her five-hundred-dollar-a-day appetite.

When police booked Stacey Smith into jail, they registered her as Daisey Ellen Riley. And until she was on the witness stand in 1993, no one, not even her lawyer, knew any different.

By the time of her trial, though, Stacey had latched onto the Lord (and the Lord onto her), and she didn't want to swear on the Word of the Lord to tell nothing but the truth and then lie about her name. But she did.

From the witness stand, however, she looked at Judge John Holland and said: "This is not my name."

Judge Holland, retired and living in Fort Smith, says that was the first and only time in his courtroom that a suspect had voluntarily admitted to an alias.

"She was eager to get that straightened out," he said when I reached him by telephone.

In 1996, the Department of Correction changed her record to Daisey/Stacey Riley/Smith.

Some of her former prison neighbors still call the chaplain Daisey, which is okay by Stacey, because she knows who she is: "I'm back to who I really am."

~ July 22, 2010

The Shortcut

The trip was the last after a day of hauling furniture in the back of the family pickup, and JoEllyn Cunning's beloved piano was the last piece of furniture to go.

JoEllyn, a sixth-grader, wasn't happy about leaving Lonoke, but her parents had bought a general store twenty miles away in Ward.

And at the moment, she wasn't happy about putting the piano in the back of the truck. Her piano was the Cunnings' nicest piece of furniture, a low-riding mahogany spinet with a mirror inlaid over the black and whites.

JoEllyn was five when she started piano and voice lessons. Bud and Clara Mae Cunning bought the piano when she was ten, a combination birthday and Christmas present. The Cunnings' customers would ask her to play the piano, which stood in the apartment attached to the store.

On that night in the summer of 1947, JoEllyn pleaded for permission to ride in the back of the truck, but the piano was roped securely, and her father assured her he would drive carefully.

The Cunnings — father, mother, two sons and daughter — crowded into the cab of the truck. Chuck Cunning, a first-grader, fell asleep.

Dark had fallen as Bud navigated the mostly unpaved roads to Ward. He turned off Arkansas 31 and took a sharp turn onto fresh gravel.

The truck slid in the loose rock, and Chuck awoke to the noise of the piano tumbling out of the truck. The piano lay in hundreds of pieces, moonlight reflecting off shards of mirror. Father and sons picked up what they could while mother and daughter sobbed in the truck.

Bud was quiet the rest of the trip, regretful that he took the shortcut.

A month later, a used piano arrived from Searcy. "The keys were worn from years of playing. Many deep scratches shone through heavy coats of furniture wax," Chuck Cunning wrote in his book, A Son of Lonoke.

"JoEllyn looked at it momentarily then covered her face and ran to her room. Mother looked at Daddy and said, 'She'll be okay.'

"Later that night, after everyone had gone to sleep, I was awakened by a low plinking sound. ... It was my sister, sitting at the piano quietly playing, 'Shine on ... Shine on Harvest Moon...'"

JoEllyn's piano story doesn't end there, though. On her twenty-fifth birthday, her husband surprised her with a new piano, a mahogany spinet, which, for now, one of her two daughters is keeping for her in Ward.

JoEllyn Cunning Moore lives with her other daughter in Sherwood and still plays the piano for churches and at nursing homes.

The loss of her piano taught her a couple of lessons.

"That proves you shouldn't ever be that sentimental over anything," she says. "It can be taken away from you. It's temporary."

In the forty-two years since her late husband gave her the piano, she has moved it about four times, and that is when she makes use of the other lesson she learned.

"I always hire a piano mover."

~ October 17, 2004

Time between friends is nothing

ARKADELPHIA — In the way that friends can, we talked as if we had last visited a month ago instead of a lifetime ago.

My last trip here was in July 1976, the day Dorothy and W.A. Harkrider buried their son, Larry. We hadn't visited or even spoken since she and W.A. stopped to see me at Louisiana Tech in 1977.

Since we last spoke in person, Dorothy

Harkrider has watched three grandsons grow up. Since we last spoke, she has buried W.A.

For most of the time I was in regular contact with them, I was a kid, beginning when the Harkriders moved in across Edgewood Drive from us in Louisiana. I was in the second grade, Larry the third.

Larry and I were comrades in arms, our plastic Tommy guns burping from the cover of pines and skinny sweetgum. We slept in Larry's back yard and fried eggs for breakfast. We read Hardy Boys mysteries and attended Sunbeams at church. Larry, a country boy, taught me to say things such as: "You couldn't carry a tune in a bucket."

Once in a while I had the privilege of eating Mrs. Harkrider's chocolate-gravy biscuits for breakfast in their kitchen.

They moved back to Arkansas in time for Larry to start junior high.

I moved to Arkansas in mid-2003, but I didn't call Mrs. Harkrider until a couple of months ago. (Though I'm old enough, and she wouldn't care, I can't bring myself to call her Dorothy).

When we talked for the first time after almost a quarter of a century, Mrs. Harkrider's voice, her laugh in the telephone receiver, were as familiar as a quarter of an hour ago.

And when we visited at her dinner table, we resumed conversation as if we had simply moved from living room to kitchen, not from one stage of life to the next.

Days after our visit, though, I calculated that I'm three years older now than she was the last time we talked.

Our four hours of conversation veered seamlessly from present to past and back, and when there was a pause, it was only to take a breath.

I showed off pictures of my daughters, and she talked me out of a picture of my parents. She has scattered throughout her neat house pictures of her daughters, her sons-in-law and her grandsons.

And from a shelf in her living room, she took a portrait of Larry in his Army dress uniform. Larry, who died a month after his twentieth birthday.

"I almost didn't get over it," Mrs. Harkrider said. "For a year, I cried all the time."

Larry had been stationed at Fort Hood, Texas. In early July 1976, he had spent a week at home. On the morning of July 17, a Saturday, the Harkriders learned that Larry had died in a car crash at about three a.m. after working late. He left the base in a thunderstorm and apparently fell asleep. He crossed the center line of the highway and crashed head-on into another car, whose driver survived.

We stopped talking only because of the time, and there was still one thing that I wanted to do before I returned to Little Rock. I missed a turn, though, and instead of finding the cemetery where Larry was buried, I ended up on a road that overlooks the dam at DeGray Lake. So I took a moment at the dam, pondered the last four hours and the last twenty-seven years as the water roared through an outlet in the dam, rushing at the speed of time.

~ October 24, 2004

The name is Sorrows

Louise Sorrows hears one comment about her last name more than any other, the gist of which is: What an unusual name. Did you drown them all?

Speaking alphabetically, Louise Sorrows married up from her Italian maiden name, Zarlingo, which sentenced her to the back of every classroom save one. In high school, she recalls, an English teacher arranged her students in reverse order.

Ray Sorrows, brother of Louise's late husband Richard, is a retired FBI agent who now does investigations and background checks for corporations.

"There's a lot of [sorrows] around, but not many with the name," he says, not sorrowfully but with a chuckle.

"When I was in the bureau, I brought a lot of sorrows to people who violated the law."

It's a name people don't forget. Ray recalls that once in Detroit he encountered the agent who conducted the background check before the FBI hired him.

"I remember you," he told Ray. "I remember what that town marshal said. 'Those Sorrows boys don't cause any trouble, but they don't take anything off anybody.'"

The most grief he has ever taken for his name, says Tom Sorrows, Ray's son, is that his friends called him Tom Sawyer a lot.

Margaret Sorrows teaches journalism at Bryant High School. Students and other teachers call her "sorry Sorrows." (She didn't say whether they call her that to her face.)

"It's a distinctive name," she says. "Everybody who doesn't know me, I have to spell it for them. They want to spell it S-O-R-R-E-L-S."

A check of Switchboard.com on the Internet turned up seventy-four Sorrows in sixteen states (although some were listed twice), twenty-two of them in Arkansas. Most of them were in the South. Nine Sorrows are listed in the white pages of the Little Rock phone book, and all of them are related, Ray says.

I found one woman in Georgia whose name is Joy Sorrows.

"Yeah, it's funny," she said, not so joyfully, as she talked to me on her cell phone while she was extracting her son from her car.

I left a lot of messages on answering machines around the country. Most of the nation's Sorrows, it seems, are out during the day.

My conversations with the Sorrowses led me to see what other emotions people are named for. I found a bunch of Sorrow (singular), Sorry (two), Cry (forty-four of them), one Crying in Houma, Louisiana, and in other places Weep, Whine, Sad, Grief, Grieve, Mourn and Mourning.

On a happier note, I found Laugh, Laughter, Giggle, Giggleman (five in Arkansas), Snicker, Snigger, Happy (including one Bea Happy and one Angel Happy), Giddy and Joy, five of whom are listed as Joy Joy.

Louise Sorrows, a teller with Arvest Bank in Maumelle, was a ninth-grader when she met her man Sorrows at the Majestic Theater in Stuttgart, where she was employed. "I was working at the concession stand and took up tickets when the man of my life walked in," she says. "He bought popcorn."

~ October 19, 2004

This seemed all wrong but there they were in the produce section, sweet potatoes shrink-wrapped for microwaving.

One potato led to two, however, and after I defied nature by microwaving shrink-wrapped potatoes, I still prefer them baked in an oven or nestled in red-hot coals.

But in a pinch, the microwavables from Ridgeview Farms are a fine alternative.

For aficionados of sweet potatoes, this is a win-Wynne situation. Our tater tale takes us to Wynne in Cross County, where Terris and Kim Matthews own and operate Ridgeview Farms and produce enough sweet potatoes in a season to keep aficionados in sweet potatoes the year round.

The Matthews family grows more sweet potatoes than any other outfit in Arkansas, says Rick Wimberley, Cross County's extension agent-staff chair.

Terris and Kim owe their marriage to the orange root.

Kim was working in Jackson, Tennessee, buying for grocery stores, when she contacted the Matthews operation. Kim's telephone conversations with Terris led to taters and tots — Jaylie, ten, and Taycie, eight.

"My mother had been praying for me to meet the right person, and Terris had to be the right one. I couldn't have found him otherwise."

Terris is the fourth generation of Matthews to raise sweet potatoes, and to honor his potato predecessors, and in a show of optimism for their daughters, he and Kim have branded their potatoes Fifth Generation. The tots whose photograph graces the Fifth Generation logo are Jaylie and Taycie.

Their photograph is on boxes, plastic bags and shrink-wrapped microwaveable potatoes all over Arkansas, North America, Holland and the United Kingdom.

Ridgeview Farms has been shrink-wrapping for a year with a wrapper that will wrap thirty-eight potatoes per minute.

Kim prefers the old-fashioned baking, but she will eat the modern version when short on time, usually during her lunch break.

"If I'm at home," she says, "they're going in the oven."

As for the microwaved potato, she says, and I can confirm this, the texture and the taste are fine. "But you're speeding up the process," she says. "The sugars don't have time to crystallize and turn into syrup ..."

Terris and Kim and their daughters eat the potatoes just about any way you can fix them — french-fried, boiled, even raw, like carrot sticks.

She candies them for Terris, which is his favorite way to eat a potato.

She gave me her recipe for candied potato and summed it up like this: "It makes them not healthy."

~ April 10, 2011

Family News

ATKINS — The headlines, written seventy years apart, differ only in the number of the dead. The front-page headline in the May 27, 1938, edition of *The Atkins Chronicle* tells of an event mostly forgotten except by those who lived through it:

Two killed, Several Injured by Tornado Near Here Sunday

Sixty-nine years and nine months later, this was the headline at the top of the February 6, 2008, edition of the weekly:

Tornado devastates Atkins; Four residents die, many injured

The 1938 tornado plowed almost the same path as the one in 2008, *The Atkins Chronicle* recounted last week. Barbara Schneider, sixty-four, and Frank Reckenger, sixty, died in the '38 storm just east of the spot where three members of the Cherry family died in February.

As the members of the Chronicle's staff worked on the story last month, they didn't realize immediately that they were reporting a replication of history.

"Billy Hicks, who had lived down in that area, tipped me off that there had been another one," says Van A. Tyson, editor and publisher of the paper. "A guy came in [Monday] who was in [the tornado when] he was thirteen years old."

That fellow is the star of Van's column this week.

And there is another element of this history that repeats itself.

In 1938, Van's father, Van Tyson, was editor and manager of the newspaper. He wrote the story about the storm.

The 2008 edition of Van Tyson, seventy-years old and editor and publisher, wrote the story about this storm, and his younger sister, Beckie Tyson, wrote the headline and the opening paragraph.

Son and daughter retracing their father's trail.

"That happened on my first birthday," Van says. "May 22, 1938."

The Atkins Chronicle has been in the Tyson family for sixty of the past ninety-one years. The newspaper has occupied the same building since the late nineteen-teens.

G.L. Parker founded the paper in November 1894. Ardis Tyson, Van and Beckie's grandfather, bought it in 1917 and sold it to Van the grandson in 1959.

Van sold it to Thomas Gillespie in 1961 and bought it back in 1992.

The paper remains a family outfit. Ginnie, Van's wife, is the business manager and co-publisher. She often contributes stories and photographs. Beckie Tyson is the managing editor. Gail Tyson Murdoch, Van's daughter, is the contributing editor, son-in-law Mark Murdoch is the office manager. Mark's nephew Zack Murdoch, eighteen, is the assistant Webmaster.

Though the office has modern equipment, it's not far removed from its past. The back room is a rag-tag museum of sorts that includes Van's grandfather's chair. The most impressive artifact is the Model 14 Linotype, which sits dusty at the very back.

When Van was eleven, his grandfather launched him into the business as a printer's devil, and he set type on the Linotype.

"If you set a line too tight," he recalls in a voice of experience, "it squirted molten lead on your left ankle."

This is newspapering as it was meant to be, reporting the big storms and the chicken-spaghetti potlucks, newspapering that will keep newspapers alive, newspapering little changed from the last century except that now it's easier on left ankles.

~ **March 20, 2008**

This notice appeared in the Arkansas Democrat *on June 26, 1981: "Publicity and the apprehension of two teen-aged suspects have 'pretty much stopped' the killings of government-protected little blue herons and cattle egrets at a nesting area on Springhill Road near Bryant, according to Andrew Pursley of the federal Fish and Wildlife Service's Enforcement Division at Little Rock." Twenty-three years later:*

The tough man who protected little blue herons walks with two canes now. He times his meals to level his blood sugar. He rarely goes anywhere, but when he does, he occasionally forgets where he is or where he is going.

Which is a change for Andy Pursley.

For most of his working life as an agent of the U.S. Department of the Interior, Andy Pursley was on the go and knew where he was going. To Canada to band ducks. To Louisiana to catch alligator poachers. To Atlanta to commandeer a planeload of illegal alligator hides. To the land of Deliverance, Georgia, to arrest a fugitive whose meanness had immobilized the local sheriff.

The first time I met the tough man, in the spring of 2004, Andy was living in the house he had bought thirty years ago. His daughter was fretting that he ought to live in a retirement home, but Pursley was not having any of that.

He was tough enough to care for himself. By himself.

Symbols of a tough man abounded in that house. A custom-made knife. A custom-made, Goliath-size slingshot by the front door. A revolver.

"I've been carrying a gun for fifty-eight years," he said. "I ain't going to quit now."

From his days as a federal agent, he carries in his billfold a badge, which flashes when he pulls out folding money.

The tough man, a Tennessean born in 1928 and retired in west Little Rock, laughs easily. But often his smiles draw down into a look of sadness, and he cries, a mixed message as if his heart is at odds with itself, which is what a stroke will do for you.

He tells of the day he pulled another agent from a Tennessee lake with a case of the bends. He cries when he tells it: "I get torn up every time I think about it."

Wasn't afraid of anybody, he says, which my Uncle Tom, who worked with Andy in Tennessee, confirms.

His early life, Andy says, made him tough. His father, a hot-tempered man who played piccolo and flute with John Philip Sousa, abandoned his family when Andy was two. "I try not to hate him," he says.

After our first meeting, I didn't see Andy for two months. I called to invite him out for lunch. I picked him up on the day he turned seventy-six.

But not at his house.

I picked him up at the retirement community where he now lives. Without a gun. Which, obviously, is a change for the tough man.

At lunch at Franke's, he tricked our waitress out of a kiss on the cheek. "A woman who hasn't been kissed in five minutes is going to waste," he says.

After lunch, in a toad-strangling rain, we drove to his house where we had first met. Cabinet doors from his kitchen covered the garage floor, where a fellow he had never seen warned us to be careful of the wet paint. Inside the house, where he had lived for thirty years, the carpet was gone. The walls of the den were bare, the fireplace mantel empty.

He knew this was going to happen. He had given the house to his daughter. But he learned the actual fact from the painter: Someone already had bought his house. His daughter, careful of his fragile emotions, hadn't found the right time to tell him.

He asked permission to use the bathroom, his bathroom. Then we walked to my Jeep for the return to his retirement home.

"That's a fine note," he muttered, looking into the garage, rain soaking his shirt and running in streaks down his cheeks.

~ August 24, 2004

I met Andy Pursley at the urging of my Uncle Tom Grelen, who worked with him in the Tennessee wildlife agency. Andy died October 9, 2005.

After 98 years, who cares?

They don't know which of the twins is older. "We never asked," says Carolyn Siebenmorgan. But Carolyn acted the elder. "She used to boss me around," says Carl Hoelzeman, who was sitting in a chair within smacking distance of his sister.

They were sitting in the living room of the house that Carl built for Carolyn and her husband. In 1952. This house, off H Street in Little Rock, is the only place Carolyn has lived.

They didn't ask about their times of arrival when they could, and they sure don't care now. But they have kept track of what happened and when since then.

Carl, who earned his living building houses, built Carolyn's fifty-six years ago. Carl was forty-two years old when he built it.

Add it or subtract it, however you do the math, you find out that these twins have been twins for a while. Two years shy of a century.

On August 7, the twins celebrated their ninety-eighth birthday, which makes them the oldest surviving twins I've ever known by about half a century. The oldest twins of my acquaintance previously were the brothers who ran the Twin W produce stand at the big flea market in Mobile, Alabama. At fifty-one, they were still young.

They can't guarantee this fact, but they may be the oldest surviving twins in Arkansas. I couldn't find any others.

The oldest known twins in the world, at least as of last year, are Canadians Ellen Robertson and Sarah Jeanmougin, who made one-hundred-and-five in May 2007.

Carolyn and Carl arrived at Sardis Crossing in 1910, the fourth and fifth of six children born to Henry and Mary (Riedmiller) Hoelzeman.

Of course they were born at home, Carl says: "We didn't have no hospital."

Their father farmed, and so, then, did they. He grew cotton, peaches, pears, strawberries, which they picked and delivered to the packing sheds. They milked their cows and raised chickens for eggs and Sunday lunch.

Carl plowed with a mule.

"I was always glad," he says, "to see winter come."

They lived on a hundred-twenty acres two miles east of Morrilton. They walked the railroad tracks every day into town, where they attended Sacred Heart school.

After they finished school, which only went through the eighth grade, Carl learned to build from his Uncle Frank, and Carolyn eventually moved to Little Rock, where she worked as a housekeeper and sold Schneider's chocolates from their counter at Second and Main and later out of the Blass department store at Park Plaza, right below the escalator.

The Army drafted Carl at thirty-two, but he remained stateside because he had put out an eye chopping kindling when he was fourteen.

Carolyn was forty-two before she married, Carl was forty-six.

Now they are nearly one-hundred years old.

Carl moved into a nursing home three months ago. He takes no medicine. Carolyn, who has survived cancers of the skin and breast, still drives, but only to church and the grocery.

The twins swapped information as they spoke of their lives, both sharp on the long-ago, Carl not so much on the more recent.

"We just had that one light hanging down the middle," Carl says, remembering when electricity came to Sardis Crossing. "Who wired that house for us anyway?"

As kids, the matter of their simultaneous births, which was a surprise to their parents when Doc Logan pulled out the second one, hardly affected their lives.

"I'm sure," Carolyn says, "we didn't dress alike."

~ September 28, 2008

Carolyn died May 14, 2010, three months shy of her one-hundredth birthday. Carl died October 22, 2012. He was one-hundred-and-two.

Who you callin' Mister Disaster?

Jim Burnett didn't get where he is by answering bone-headed questions such as the one I had just posed.

Jim, a country lawyer from Clinton, which is a suburb of Damascus, is famous and much-sought after for his insight into travel safety because for nearly a decade, he ran the National Transportation Safety Board.

Although he has been out of the job longer than he was in it, national newspapers still quote him, and national television news shows still broadcast his thoughts after national transportation disasters such as a plane crash or the collapse of a bridge.

He has kept this high and respected profile for decades because he knows when to quit talking.

Before Jim was a nationally famous safety guy, he was a judge in Clinton, where he grew up and where he lives with his mother in the house where his parents raised him.

After his nearly ten years with the federal safety commission during the Reagan and Bush Sr. years, Jim resumed his role as a country lawyer, a description and a job he likes just fine.

I met Jim twenty years ago in Denver, where I was a reporter for *The Denver Post*. He came to town to investigate the crash of Continental Flight 1713 in November 1987.

He was constantly on TV — coat, tie, red suspenders, fancy walking stick — with updates about the crash, which killed twenty-eight people.

I followed him everywhere he went for a couple of days, and I wrote a story that included quotes from his mother back in Clinton, where he occasionally retreated to escape the bright lights. "He'll maybe sleep late and rest a day, and then walk to town and make the rounds," she told me then, which I know because I still have a copy of the story.

With his name showing up in the news again after the recent bridge collapse in Minneapolis, I telephoned him to renew our acquaintance. Needless to say, I remembered him better than he remembered me. By which I mean, he had no recollection whatsoever of me.

As timing would have it, Jim already was planning a trip to Little Rock. The next week, I picked him up at his hotel, and we went to the west Little Rock Corky's.

So there I was, polishing off my pintos and hoping to make news by asking him a newsmaking question. Jim thoughtfully picked his at a plate of fried catfish.

As we picked through his career and his memory of the Denver disaster, he suddenly recalled: "One of the Denver papers called me Mister Disaster. They even put it in the headline."

That sounded real familiar to me.

"Did you, um, like that?" I asked tentatively.

"I did at first," he says, "but then I thought maybe that wasn't so good."

"I think that was my story," I admitted.

(I later found the clipping. I was, indeed, the one who first called him Mister Disaster.)

So anyway, we're sitting at Corky's, I'm on my third glass of sweet tea, and I have this question to ask, and then I'm thinking about the potential power of simple words.

I am intrigued to think that news-making industry-shaking words could come from such an unpretentious fellow in such an innocent and everyday Southern setting as a barbecue joint with diners all around.

"So," ask I, "... is there an airline you refuse to fly because it's unsafe? Or is there one ... that you always fly?"

Well, he tells me in his country-lawyer way, a long time ago he wouldn't fly U.S. Air, and United once was one of his favorites because of the superior training of airline employees.

Before I realize he has changed the subject, we are talking about his current work. He has danced me right past my attempt to make news. In his country-lawyer way, Mr. Disaster finished his catfish and never answered my question.

~ **August 12, 2007**

• • • • •

CLINTON — The pictures in the outer office tell only part of the story of Jim Burnett's career.

They are the pictures of him smiling, shaking hands with the likes of the first President Bush and other very important people in Washington.

It's the other photographs, the ones back in Mr. Burnett's work room, that fill in the rest of his story.

And Mr. Burnett is not in any of those. They are the photographs of tragedy and catastrophe, the focus of Mr. Burnett's nearly ten years in D.C.

Those pictures show a small plane nosed into the front of a two-story house, a train derailed, a commercial jet crashed. Some of the accidents made national news, some were only local.

For the years he served as chairman of the National Transportation Safety Board, these were the scenes from his work.

And although he has been home in Arkansas for nearly twice as long as he was with the NTSB, whenever a plane crashes or a bridge collapses, newspaper and TV reporters with national news organizations still call him for comment at his law office and at home.

"I've been interviewed a lot of times in my underwear," he says, and then drops the names of cable TV personalities Larry King and Greta Van Susteren.

On Monday, a crew from The Weather Channel will tape an interview with him about a 1982 plane crash.

Mr. Burnett happened to be in Minneapolis the day of the bridge collapse. His secretary, Dixie Lee Carter, and his mother at home fielded a hundred telephone calls while he was driving back to Arkansas.

"That's why I don't have a cell phone," he says. "I can't [ignore] a ringing phone, and I can't talk and drive."

Many well-known tragedies occurred during Mr. Burnett's terms on the NTSB, starting with the crash of an Air Florida jet into a bridge over the Potomac River less than two weeks after he started the job in January 1982 and a crash in Kenner, Louisiana, in July that year.

Other investigations that he oversaw for the NTSB include the explosion of the when the Challenger space shuttle; the 1985 crash at the Dallas-Fort Worth airport that focused attention on the role of wind-shear in crashes; the crash and oil spill in Alaska of the Exxon Valdez.

He came into office in the wake of the strike by air traffic controllers that Ronald Reagan famously cut short.

In 1994, Mr. Burnett was foreman of the federal grand jury that indicted Judge David Hale.

Now he practices law in the rock-walled building where his father owned a dry-goods store. He has his pictures, and he has his books, hundreds of them on subjects ranging from English law to the Civil War to multiple volumes of Will Durant's *The Story of Civilization*.

An umbrella holder, wedged between his roll-top desk and a bookshelf, holds a dozen walking canes, which he needs because of a flying-related back injury.

He is most proud of his work to raise the drinking age nationally in hopes of reducing the number of alcohol-related traffic accidents.

One piece of unfinished business that troubles him is what he says is inadequate direction for pilots coming and going on runways.

"I am most nervous," he says, "about an accident on the ground."

~ **August 19, 2007**

Where Cut Off Creek flows into Seven Devils Swamp

COLLINS — The water is murkier than it was in the days when Joe Sasser and Bud Bulloch swam here. Cypress knees now protrude in places they didn't, and the cypress trees scratch the sky. The beach no longer is sandy.

Fifty years will do that to a place.

They took me to their swimming hole, these former boys, and to the other places around this weed-grown town where they romped in their cowboy boots and broke out windows with rocks.

"We thought we'd done something pretty good," says Bud, recalling that his father wasn't favorably impressed when they reported that they had taken care of the glass fragments in his great-grandfather's abandoned store.

They were friends before they started school, this pair, and they have lived their lives, and they remain friends. Bud saw the world. Joe stayed close. They talk several days a week.

There was the corner where Joe and his family lived in their gas station, and over there, the train tracks once cut through. The brick streets didn't have names, then, except everyone knew Main Street, which ran past the three-room school.

Joe's father hung the church bell, and when they tore down the church, his daddy salvaged it.

"The old man who taught me how to box was a blacksmith," Joe says. "He was short but muscular." His name was Frank "Lyin' " Burns.

They rode horses through these woods, went a'courtin' horseback through these woods.

"I threw the *Democrat* from my horse," Joe says.

Bud drives us to the cemetery, and they stroll the graves and tell the stories you tell at cemeteries. Bud helped Joe pick out his father's casket.

The final destination of our tour was this swimming hole in Cut Off Creek, which runs into Bayou Bartholomew.

A friend had bush-hogged the path so we could drive, but back then, this had been a path for bare feet, and back then, the water brimmed with bream, catfish, crappie, and the water was cold enough to chill the watermelons they stole.

One night Joe's Uncle John heard Joe in his watermelon patch and fired his Model 97 Winchester shotgun into the briars, Joe hollering his uncle's name for mercy. Joe, a melon under each arm, was hugging dirt, his bare arms and legs an all-you-can-eat for the mosquitos.

This was the town where the boys came to Jesus, and this swimming hole was the place where the preacher dunked Joe.

Bud's dunking was more civilized, in the Baptist church in Dermott, with its baptismal pool in the sanctuary.

"I'd never been to a church with a baptistry," Bud says. "The curtains drew back. ... I thought I was seeing a vision. 'This is a vision of heaven.'"

Joe's salvation came in a hay field, right on a bale of hay, during the week of revival in town.

"It was some shouting that night," he says, and he tells about the baptism in Cut Off Creek, which runs out of Seven Devils Swamp.

"You get baptized in a place like this," Bud says, "you got to have religion."

All over their old town, they notice the little things — barbed wire where there wasn't any just a year ago, a tree gone.

"Kind of looks different, Joe," Bud says. "Fifty years — is that what's different?"

~ July 27, 2008

The Fuller Hardware boys

Now that young J.R. has joined his father, Bobby, and brother, Jeff, in the hardware business, oughtn't they add an "s" to Fuller & Son?

It's a question that they discussed after J.R. signed on this year as a member of the fourth generation of Fullers to sell hardware in Little Rock.

Walter "Pop" Fuller started his business in

1921 as Fuller Feed & Supply, which evolved to Fuller Hardware & Feed to the current Fuller & Son Hardware, which was an accurate name until the end of May.

Walter "Happy" Fuller bought the business from Pop in 1946 upon his return from the war, and Bobby kept it in the family when he bought it from Happy in 1985.

There was a brief moment, though, that Happy wasn't certain that anyone from the third generation would carry on.

Three of his sons already had decided on other careers and declined his offer to sell. Bobby, Happy's last hope, was traveling as the leader of Bobby Fuller and the Fuller Brothers, although he was the only family member still in the band, which was their mother's brainstorm.

"My mother one time saw three little girls singing, and she thought, 'I have four boys,'" Bobby says. So when he was about six, she put her four sons into singing lessons, and before it was over, they could play twenty-eight musical instruments among them and were performing around the country.

They opened for performers like Bob Hope, Robert Goulet, Perry Como, Florence Henderson, Phyllis Diller, Jimmy Dean, Eddy Arnold and Louie Armstrong, who offered them this show-biz advice: "Get your money and get out of town."

They released at least four forty-five RPMs (Bobby can't remember exactly) through Decca, Capitol and Monument records. Their big hit, which made it onto the Top 100 in the 1960s, was "Big Church Wedding."

Wedding by wedding, though, baby by baby, career by career, the brothers dropped out until Bobby was the last brother standing.

It was in 1985, as Happy prepared to retire, that he offered the business to his sons. Although he thought he knew the answer, Happy called Bobby, who was performing in Dallas.

"He said he knew I wasn't interested, but he wanted to ask," Bobby says. "I said, 'You know, I think I will.'"

So Bobby and Carolyn and their young sons retired from the road, a decision he has never regretted.

"The pay may be poor," he says, "but at least the hours are grueling."

The original store at 28th and Arch is vacant. Now they compete against the "big boxes," the national warehouse-size hardware stores, with five stores and a promise to match any price in town.

Most importantly, though, Bobby Fuller wants to honor his father and grandfather and the reputation they built.

"People talk about my dad, what a good man, honest man, he was," he says and pauses, tears brimming. "I want that too."

So in the end, Fuller and sons have decided to leave the name of the business Fuller & Son, singular, which, translated, means Pop & Happy Hardware, a pretty good name for a business.

~ October 5, 2004

Counting grandkids, there are a whole bunch of Duggars

The population of Duggar qualifies the family for a spot on the Arkansas map.

They are up to nineteen children, one daughter-in-law and a granddaughter.

Assuming each child marries, and supposing each new family follows the path of Jim Bob and Michelle, at a population of four-hundred-twenty, the Duggar clan could incorporate and start its own police and fire departments.

Except the family wouldn't need police.

I have never watched the Duggars' television show, *19 Kids and Counting*.

I have, however, observed them when the TV crew wasn't around, and, if Duggar was a village, I'd want to live there. If the children behave any better on camera than they do in real life, the people who rate TV will have to invent a rating more tame than a G.

Consider church. I visited Friendly Chapel the Sunday that Michelle and Jim Bob told their story.

Everyone but three-month-old Josie, who was living at Arkansas Children's Hospital, was there, even Aunt Josie's five-month-old niece. (Did you catch that? At three-months of age, Josie is aunt of a five-month-old niece.) The children, exceeding in number the von Trapp Family Singers, opened the service, singing and performing on violins and a harp.

As kids will, the younger ones squirmed and drew and looked around while their parents spoke, but you'd hardly know the pews held six siblings who were eight years old or younger.

Another day, I observed four of the older daughters as they helped set up a clothing sale in Friendly Chapel's gym. They worked as steadily as everyone else; upon finishing one task, they found another without prompting. No star behavior there.

The day I first met them, though, was the best.

Paul Holderfield, pastor at Friendly Chapel, took me to the house they rented while prematurely born Josie stayed at Children's Hospital. Jim Bob showed Paul and me around the ninety-something-year-old eight-thousand-square-foot mansion, where some of the children played in a fort and others worked at a desk full of computers. And the younger Duggar children stayed with us, darting mouse-like around Jim Bob's feet, racing up the stairs ahead of him, their noise level never above cheerful playground chatter.

Cheerful is a good description. Their interaction and good comportment is cheerful and spontaneous, not the compelled good behavior of the movie-version von Trapp children who wilted under the baron's horsewhip and whistle.

In one room, Jim Bob showed us the harp the family purchased at an estate sale in Springdale (they bid against someone calling from Germany), and we persuaded Jill and Jana to play.

We sat in the sparsely furnished antique parlor, Jim Bob, Paul and I, the three o'clock sun of an early March afternoon speckling the walls, the high-ceilinged room devoid of anything obviously modern – the calendar might have read 1910. The notes of Pachelbel's "Canon in D" fluttered from Jana's fingers, slipping through the beams of sun, peace in the bosom of a family, the fair village of Duggar.

~ August 5, 2010

SEARCY — Leister Presley cut up his Cloie's letters first, two-hundred of them, snip-snip-snip one direction, then snip-snip crossways so that only one-inch squares remained.

The project took half a day, and the scraps filled a trash bag.

Three or four days later, Leister dug out the two-hundred or so letters he had written out of a footlocker. Another half a day, another trash bag.

Then he hauled it all to the recycling plant and poured the shreds of their two-year courtship into the grinder along with their old bank statements.

"I felt like it was something that needed to be done," he says. "I didn't think anybody had any business reading them. She's not here anymore. And I'll be gone ..."

They were married fifty-six years, though she didn't know him for the last two, which she spent in a nursing home, laid low by Alzheimer's.

"I went and saw her every day. I missed two days in two-oh-oh-four going to see her. I missed a few days in two-oh-oh-three. I did the best I could."

He was with her when she died, not the first time he'd accompanied a beloved woman at the last.

He was nine years old the first time, and his brother was seven. They were spending the night with their grandparents and didn't know that in their own house, their mother was giving birth to a third son.

When the doctor realized he couldn't stanch Maggie's bleeding, he suggested to their father, Luther, that he summon the boys. Their mother was twenty-seven.

"She knew us. She put her arms around us and told us to be good. She died before daylight."

They buried their little brother in the coffin with their mother.

"Dad, he was worst tore up than anybody I ever saw."

• • • • •

They met at church, Cloie and Leister. For two years after that, she taught school in Garner and he worked for Arkansas Power & Light twenty miles away in Searcy. During the school year, they wrote two, three letters apiece every week. They married in August 1948.

In November, Cloie went into the hospital with pneumonia. All day November 12, Leister stayed with her. Her brother came that night. They all slept until early November 13, when Cloie's brother awakened Leister because she was breathing erratically.

"At 4 o'clock," he says, "she quit breathing."

• • • • •

Awhile back, Leister bought a double headstone for their graves, which are next to his mother's. But Cloie died before the monument company set the stone over their plot. Leister called the company to give them Cloie's date of death. He was worried they might charge more for the extra engraving.

Leister's father composed more than a thousand hymns. His most famous songs are "When the Saints Go Marching In" and "I'd Rather Have Jesus." Friends have told Leister that his father was thinking of Maggie when he wrote "Will Someone Be Waiting."

Leister is ninety-two. His mother, his stepmother, his wife and his father have preceded him, and he is ready to be in their number. He knows they are waiting.

~ January 23, 2005

Leister Presley died September 4, 2009.

MISSISSIPPI COAST — The silence here is primitive, the silence of a thousand years ago, the civilized silence before civilization intruded.

No dogs wandering, no cats. Three months after Hurricane Katrina, locals report that the gulls and the pelicans haven't returned to the west end. Animal life is limited to the occasional yellow-winged butterfly, an occasional dragonfly.

The human population along the shoreline has been reduced to the occasional survivor living in a tent or a trailer, the occasional sightseer.

The destruction, of course, isn't limited to the coast. The federal government declared all eighty-seven of Mississippi's counties disaster areas, with forty-seven suffering "significant" damage to homes, businesses and to public infrastructure such as roads, power lines and water supplies.

"This is the vast untold story about Mississippi," says Buddy Bynum, Governor Haley Barbour's spokesman. "It's hard to explain to people who haven't seen it."

And even for those who have been here, the numbers boggle: two-hundred-thirty-one people dead, with five bodies still unidentified; sixty-seven people missing; more than sixty-five-thousand homes destroyed; eighty miles of coast development flattened.

The silence bespeaks the devastation in places such as Bay St. Louis, where gentle breezes off the Gulf tickle the branches of what's left of the live oaks and the pines, the swish slightly more audible as breezes play across the shredded plastic grocery bags and plastic sheeting that Katrina draped in trees in place of the Spanish moss she whisked away.

With a thirty-foot storm surge and fifteen-foot waves on top of that, Katrina knocked hundreds of houses off their piers. Now thousands of empty piers stand in tight clusters like ancient ruins, some in rectangular clusters, some in circular, Greek columns on the Gulf of Mexico.

Majestic curved brick staircases that led into antebellum homes now step off into nowhere, ending abruptly at the top and dropping off into piles of bricks that once made the home.

In the weeks after the storm, Governor Barbour created the Commission on Recovery, Rebuilding and Renewal to help sift through the ruins, a clearinghouse for ideas, a forum on the future.

For those hit hardest, like those in Hancock County, rebuilding is a back-burner dream as they concentrate simply on survival and recovery.

"There is very little rebuilding yet," Bynum says. "The renewal part is physical and psychological."

As homeowners recover, they are learning about things like the Right of Entry, which each must sign before the Federal Emergency Management Agency and the Army Corps of Engineers can move onto private property and clean up the mess.

On the coast, they measure progress in small ways: The Cracker Barrel restaurant in Gulfport is using ceramic plates and silverware again after serving on paper for two months because the managers couldn't hire enough people to wash dishes.

The degree of destruction increases east to west. Ocean Springs looks bad until you see Biloxi, which looks awful until you follow U.S. 90 into Long Beach. After Long Beach, the scenes of destruction are redundant and incomprehensible.

Incomprehensible and seemingly overwhelming until you narrow your view, see the coast one slab at a time, talk to one family at a time, one woman, one man, and out of the primitive bone-breaking silence, voices muffled in the howl rise in optimism.

Voices like that of David Harris, who lost his Ocean Springs house and a dry-dock business and whose son's house burned three days later: You lay back your ears like a mule at the plow, says Harris, sixty-six. "I'm always confident things will work out. Maybe I'm ignorantly optimistic."

On the eastern shore at Ocean Springs, where Tim Scarborough has an unobstructed view of Deer Island in the Mississippi Sound, his diesel-powered track excavator disrupts the silence as man and machine finish off the ninety-year-old estate that is called Shadowlawn, which, from a distance, appears to have survived Katrina unscathed.

But the house, resting on what passes here on the Gulf Coast for a hill, had its problems before Hurricane Katrina. Now the house is beyond repair. This is much like putting down an injured thoroughbred, which to the untrained and sympathetic eye, is only limping but that will never recover.

Mr. Scarborough's six-toed bucket reaches up twenty-two feet, and it claws at the roof and walls of what was a two-million-dollar peach-colored stucco house. Pine timbers crack and sound to me like the rifle salute at a soldier's grave. Glass shatters.

"You're raised up to not tear things down," Scarborough says as he takes a break. "It's breaking my heart."

Heart break is a common thing for many here, like the daughters of Walter Anderson, the painter who, legend has it, tied himself to a tree to experience Hurricane Betsy in 1965.

The truth, as his daughters tell it, is less mystical though no less captivating. The storm trapped him on Horn Island, and he rode out Betsy in his rowboat, which, Mary Anderson Pickard says, he had tied to a tree.

The Anderson family generally, and Walter Anderson specifically, gave Ocean Springs an identity, and Ocean Springs is the family's identity.

"This wasn't a good place to be," Leif Anderson says of the days after the storm. "No milk. No vegetables. Horrible, horrible black flies. Fruit flies. They were in my refrigerator. Drain flies."

"None of us has been normal," Mary says. "You have short tempers. Everything you've known is destroyed. My home from childhood is gone. It's like the end of the world."

"We don't talk about numbers," Leif says. "We've lost a lot."

• • • • •

Talk of rebuilding the coast generally follows two distinct sets of mind: The idealists want the coast to be all pink azaleas and pedestrian trails. The pragmatists want roads that provide quick evacuation and ease of movement without regard for the sensibilities of Southern Living photographers.

The first beneficiary of future-think was the state's gambling industry: Before the storm, state law allowed only floating casinos. The Legislature changed the law to allow developers to build casinos on land.

The President Casino was among the most-photographed casualties of the hurricane. The surge washed it a quarter-mile west of its moorings and dropped it atop the lobby of a two-story motel.

The week after Thanksgiving, a crew of robotics scientists from the University of South Florida flew a pint-size remote-controlled helicopter over and around the wreckage, taking pictures for engineers who build such buildings.

"This is a lot of major structural damage," says team leader Robin Murphy. "You want to know how these buildings hold up."

On the back side of the President, the motel courtyard is a square dirty sink with all manner of unexpected debris. The pool sits at the center like the drain. The water in the pool is black.

Inside the courtyard, a cacophony of haunting chirps breaks the silence — smoke detectors in empty motel rooms chirping for fresh batteries. The plate glass windows are broken out of most rooms; inside the rooms, mattresses and sofas had floated and landed in odd places and positions.

John LaBrack, who lived in Long Beach, was between jobs on August 29. Now he works for Samaritan's Purse, a nondenominational Christian relief organization.

"What you are seeing," he says, swatting at a swarm of biting no-see-um gnats, "looks great to us."

When he and his wife returned after Katrina, they couldn't find the street where they have lived for a decade. One street was indistinguishable from the next. The street signs were gone, and so were the streets. The landscape was uninterrupted debris.

"We have a slab down there," he says. "We taped our windows up before we left."

• • • • •

Nanette Carter, a real estate agent, is young enough to start over in Pass Christian, where she sold her first million-dollar home the week after Thanksgiving.

"It survived," she says. "The water came right up to the door."

Real estate is Carter's second career. Until August 29, she and her husband ran a nursery that specialized in aquatic plants.

But Katrina wiped out their downtown business as well as their house next door, which, Nanette says, gives them the chance to start a new business — a coin-operated laundry with a coffee shop/Internet cafe attached. She hopes to be the first business to launch in a reviving, if shrunken, Pass Christian.

Before Katrina, Mayor Billy McDonald says, Pass Christian's population was seven-thousand; the roll has shrunk to about twelve-hundred. More than twenty people died, and half a dozen haven't been found.

"It makes me sick," Billy Mac says. "I've lived here all my life."

The town lost nearly eighty percent of its tax base. Katrina wiped out the Wal-Mart, alone worth a million dollars annually in taxes. Last week, the mayor says, a Wal-Mart official promised the store would reopen.

Of the thirty-one-hundred homes in town, only eight hundred remain. Of the nearly eighty antebellum homes for which Pass Christian was famous, only fifteen are left. City Hall is now a double-wide trailer, as is the public library, just down from First Baptist Church, which the congregation will demolish because the waves beat holes in the walls.

Nanette is among those hoping that CSX Corporation will move its rail tracks — which haven't seen a train since Katrina — north of Interstate 10. Then, she hopes, Mississippi will obtain the right of way for a trolley system that runs from Ocean Springs to Bay St. Louis to New Orleans.

That's a billion-dollar dream, says Bynum, the governor's spokesman, but a possibility.

Three months after the flood, coils of barbed wire still line the tracks, evidence of efforts to keep looters out of town, where the water lifted houses, moved them north several feet and slammed them into the house next door, which is what happened to two homes that seventy-year-old Lottie Mae Romain owns. "Romain," she says by way of introduction, "like the lettuce."

After three months in a Gulfport shelter, which Lottie Mae calls "dope alley," she had just returned to Pass Christian to live in one of the approximately seventy military-style tents that the locals have dubbed "The Village."

Here kindness, as often as devastation, evokes emotion in survivors.

"The other day, I got a call from a florist. She had a poinsettia from a church in South Carolina that just wanted to remember our church at Christmas," says Carolyn Smith, whose husband Bill is pastor of First Baptist in the Pass. "We have been overwhelmed with donations, love. We have not asked for one donation. The media may have forgotten Mississippi, but God hasn't."

• • • • •

Stand Judi Brooks up to the waterline in her first-floor sewing room, and you see that if she hadn't moved upstairs, she would have been up to her eyebrows in seawater.

By her own testimony, Judi Brooks, who now lives in a FEMA trailer beside her house, was stupid.

But Hurricane Camille, the storm by which all storms were measured before Katrina, had stopped short of her family's property in 1969.

So at her insistence, she and her family stayed in their five-year-old house with its fine view of the beach a half-mile down Coleman Avenue.

She takes me on a tour of her house, pointing out the sky through a hole in the ceiling of the master bedroom. Much of the wallboard in the house has been torn out, and an electrician has finished the rewiring.

When the water receded five hours after it filled the Brookses' home, the mud inside was eight inches deep.

Three months later, the dirt is still evident, a fact for which Mrs. Brooks apologizes repeatedly, as she does for the general wreckage inside her house, where she points out the ruined grand piano and, in another room, her sixteen-year-old's bedroom set delivered four days before the storm and never used.

Their damage is about two-hundred-sixty-thousand dollars. Insurance isn't paying. "If I'd've had a fire," she says, "I'd be over-insured."

Like many on the coast, the Brookses didn't carry flood insurance because the maps showed, and the insurance company and FEMA concurred, that they weren't in a flood zone.

Now, like many, they are trapped between definitions. The insurance company says the water rose inside their house and therefore it was a flood. The Brookses argue that the water was driven by wind and thus was not a flood.

Inside their house, the adjuster pointed to the waterline and said: "You had water. I don't pay for anything below this."

Dickie Scruggs, a Mississippi lawyer who made his fame in lawsuits against tobacco companies, is suing insurance companies that refuse to pay water-damage claims to "homeowners who didn't have separate, federally backed flood insurance," according to *The Sun Herald* of Biloxi, Stan Tiner, editor.

Meanwhile, reports the local newspaper: "Mississippi's congressional delegation — including Scruggs' brother-in-law, Sen. Trent Lott — and Gov. Barbour are pushing for a federal bailout, saying homeowners didn't have federal flood insurance because the government told them they didn't need it."

The governor, Bynum says, thinks those people have a legitimate complaint.

"As the governor says it, a lot of people relied to their detriment on the federal government to define the flood elevations and feel like it's the government's job to make them whole."

The Brookses aren't waiting for the government or their insurance company. They are working to reopen their barbecue restaurant. Until then, they have no income.

Judi Brooks knows they are not alone.

"The ones who had a lot have nothing," she says. "The ones who had nothing have nothing. It took me thirty full days to really break down and cry. Thirty-six years married. Six, eight hours, it's all gone."

All gone but nothing that matters.

"We started out with eleven people," she says. "We ended up with eleven."

~ December 16, 2005

Cotton Nixon, his gaze glued to the violin case in my right hand, threw his legs over the side of his hospital bed, his hands homing in on the fiddle like a starving man grabbing for a supper plate.

Cotton, eighty-three and fiddling since he was eleven, hadn't had much chance to make music, as he had been laid up the VA the last couple of months.

We exchanged words enough for me to identify myself as the fellow from the newspaper, and that was all the introduction he needed.

He took the fiddle and nested it between his chin and his shoulder, quick-cut the horsehairs over the strings a couple of times, tuned the strings, and then without warning to anyone or asking permission of his roommate, the man in Room 142, Bed 18, made music.

His tongue slid back and forth between his bottom gum and lip, unimpeded by his teeth, which sat on the tray beside his bed. Then his tongue went over to his left cheek, which, without teeth for support, was sunken.

Sometimes he eyed his fingers slipping up and down the neck, sometimes his eyes locked onto mine to the point of my discomfort. I didn't know this man, but he was talking to me with a fiddle, which, when I had left my house thirty minutes earlier, had been a violin.

After two minutes, he stopped, and we conversed, first about the instrument, bought new seven years ago for my daughters and recently retired for an upgrade.

"Mine was made in Chicago a hundred-fifty years ago," he says. "I had one, a black one, I retired it — the wood in it was eight-hundred years old."

He was laid up at Fort Root thanks to a brown recluse spider, which gnawed into his left foot while he slept in April 2004. "I finally killed him. He was a big ol' spider."

He didn't go to the doctor for two days, which is why the bite plagues him still. "They were worried they were going to have to cut off my foot," he says, a fact he relates with some amusement.

To save him, the doctors had to flush his circulatory system so blood would go to his foot. To do that, they cut open his abdomen, which, with its curved railroad track of a scar, looked like a basketball cut open and laid flat.

Before Cotton became Cotton, he was Milburn Nixon, known as Mill. While he lived in Houston, he played music with Willie Nelson, who was eighteen and wore the same suit for every performance.

If Cotton has a claim on fame it is for his part in composing the fiddle-country standard "Ragg Mopp."

He was sharing a three-bucks-a-week room with Deacon Anderson in Little Rock back then, and when they wrote the song, they were, he concedes, heavily under the influence of liquid spirits.

These days, Cotton mostly performs with Steve Traywick and various musicians as the band Cotton Patch. He and Deacon will reunite October 9 for a performance in Shirley, where Cotton lives.

None of his three children followed him into the music business, which is mostly how he put bread in the pantry. "I talked them out of it," he says. "They all made something of themselves."

"R-A-G-G M-O-P-P. Ragg Mopp." He plucked and sang.

"That's about all I can do now," he says, "is fiddle around."

~ **September 13, 2005**

LESLIE — In the museum upstairs, you see the faces of the first ones to play here, the Leslie High Basketball team of 1939.

The team photograph hangs on the wall of the town museum, their faces intent on the camera, the squeak of their shoes on the floor left to the imagination.

Down below, where they once ran and shot and bounced the leather balls, another set of youngsters took to the floor to put the building to a different use.

They were gathered in the Killebrew Theater in the Old Gym for the 11th Annual Old-Time Fiddle Contest.

Old Gym has a new name — Ozark Heritage Arts Center and the Killibrew Theater was too neat, too clean for this contest. When you think fiddles and bluegrass, you don't think pristine.

The rock-wall Old Gym was a Works Progress Administration project, which the WPA finished in 1939 in time for basketball season. You can walk on a section of the wooden basketball floor, complete with the lines and painted mascot, that peeks up between the stage and the seats.

Not all the musicians were youngsters. The most grizzled was eighty-five-year-old Milburn Nixon who played with Willie Nelson in Houston when Willie owned only one suit. Most folks didn't know who Milburn was, but the adults probably knew the song that made him famous (if not rich).

Milburn, better known by his stage name of Cotton, is most known for "Ragg Mopp," a song he co-wrote with Deacon Anderson when they were renting a room for three bucks a week in Little Rock.

The spirit that moved them to write that night, Cotton admitted to me when we met a couple of years ago, came in a bottle.

This small-town contest operates in a big-town way. The three judges and the tabulator sat in a dressing room offstage, listening to the music on a speaker wired to the stage mic.

They picked three from each category. Junior: Austin Duvall (first), Josh Turner and Caleb Lawrence. (The other contestants were sisters Brittany and Monica Davanzo, Emily Turner and Joshua Watkins.)

Senior: Reg Edwards, Milburn "Ragg Mopp" Nixon and Merl Reeves.

Open: Ricky Russell, Tim Trawick and Taylor Quattlebaum.

The fiddle contest ended the way one ought to end, with all the musicians on stage playing with each other, not against.

'Twas a jam supreme. Twelve fiddles. Three guitars. Brittany Davanzo and Josh Turner played "Orange Blossom Special" as if fire ants had invaded their pants, and the whole bunch played "Ookpik," a haunting fiddle waltz, as if they all were melancholy.

Emily Turner, who is twelve, first fiddled "Ookpik" as one of her mandatory three tunes, and then, while the contestants awaited the judges' decision and jammed onto the stage, Emily's teacher coaxed the shy musician back to the microphone, and Emily waltzed the rest of them through it again, all the prettier coming off a dozen fiddles on a quiet afternoon in the Ozarks.

~ **June 19, 2007**

Ol' Mil, he could play anything

Ed Kirby hadn't seen this boy in better than fifty years, didn't know he was still alive, and out of the blue he reads a newspaper column about Milburn Nixon fiddling up in Leslie.

They grew up together, Ed and Cotton (as he's known now), in a community called Springhill, near Greenbrier. Ed called me wanting to know how to contact his old buddy.

Cotton took second place in an old-time fiddling contest last week, which was no surprise to Ed, who knew Milburn when he was a kid fiddler.

"We used to go up the road about a half-mile west to Aaron Milam's house. He was a big fiddle player, too.

"We'd go up there on Saturday nights and have a big musical. Mil's brother played the guitar.

"Ol' Mil, he could play anything. We had an old organ at our house. He'd come up there, never had a lesson, didn't know any notes, and start picking around on it. First thing you know, he was playing a tune."

The boys, who are eighty-five now, showed an early aptitude for technology when they rescued a couple of old crank telephones for their personal use. "We got us some new batteries ... ran a line from each other's house, a quarter of a mile. When I'd want to hear him fiddle, I'd ring him up. He'd play his fiddle over the phone."

Ed was a high-tech kid in a home that couldn't keep out the weather.

"I'd wake up in the mornings and have it snowing in my face," he says. "My room was an added-on room to the original house, which was a two-roomer with a dogtrot down the middle."

Last week, Ed rang Cotton up for the first time in half a century. The conversation brought back other memories for Ed, like the day he and Cotton picked a peck of blackberries and decided to turn them into wine.

"I fixed me a half-gallon jar of blackberries. Put sugar in them, put in a rag, hid them in the old tin around the hog pen. My daddy, he decided he'd get out there and clean up around the pen. I come home, and before I even got around to the back, I could smell that stuff. He'd found it and poured it in the hog trough."

His parents were teetotalers (and so, now, is Ed). "He told me if he ever caught me doing that again, 'I'll whip you so hard your britches won't hold shucks.'"

Ed grew up a Missionary Baptist, and pastor W.J. Burgess baptized him at Paul Thompson's cotton gin.

"Cotton gins all had a water pool, in case they had a fire. The pool was about thirty foot square, about six or eight foot deep."

Ed lives alone in Little Rock now. Still hunts. Wishes he had learned guitar or the harmonica. But now that he knows Cotton's still kicking, he can ring him up for entertainment, the way he did when he was a high-tech kid.

Friday afternoon, he was grinding venison to mix with fat ground beef for making hamburgers. "That makes it about right," he says. "I like to charcoal them, but, if I haven't got time, I'll fry [them] in the skillet."

He makes banana pudding from scratch — bananas, a couple of eggs, a cup of sugar, a teaspoon of vanilla, couple tablespoons of flour, two cups of milk, and cooks until it thickens.

"I'm a natural-born cook," he says. "Some of my family tells me I ought've been a woman."

~ **June 24, 2007**

I have been bitten
Now I am smitten
And standin' or sittin'
For all I need written
A fountain pen
Is only fittin'

So sorry, but fountain pens have that effect on me.

This is a newly discovered love, another path to the simpler days when we wrote long eloquent letters and declarations of independence and spilled indelible ink on our frocks.

This obsession sneaked up on me after I visited Don Henderson, who had fetched home his collection of several hundred pens from a safety-deposit box. Need I say really expensive pens?

After my visit with Don, I went home and pulled out the gold-trimmed Mont Blanc a friend gave me a couple of years ago. Albert Lucas, who is a world-champion juggler (don't laugh; he's in the *Guinness Book of World Records*), delivered the pen with a bottle of ink and a soliloquy on the beauty of writing the old-fashion way.

Never mind that my actual handwriting doesn't rise to the level of hen scratch (the comparison defames the hen), and my idle doodles run the gamut from squares to rectangles drawn with crooked lines.

When I scratch or doodle with a fountain pen, however, the moments are mystical, and I tend to exaggerate even the most mundane of experiences about which I write, always careful not to dangle any "abouts" at the end of my elegant sentences.

Thus enamored, on a recent visit with my parents, I found three fifty-year-old fountain pens in Daddy's desk, which is a hollow wooden door laid across two cabinets he built decades ago. I found two Sheaffers and an Esterbrook, which was the fountain pen for blue-collar folk.

I talked them out of the Esterbrook, which wouldn't hold ink because the rubber ink bladder inside the pen barrel had dry-rotted. I know that because Van Vanness shook the pen, and the rotted old rubber bladder rattled inside the barrel, an Esterbrook mini-maraca.

So for seven bucks, Van restored a family treasure.

In Little Rock, the name Vanness means fountain pens. They know pens, and they sell the best.

Brothers Dennis and Van are the second generation to run the business, and Orville's grandson, Mike, is the third.

Two weeks ago, I went into the store as the owner of two pens. After Mike Vanness showed me the low-dollar (compared to Mont Blanc and Waterman but not compared to Bic) Safari fountain pen by Lamy (the one that nine out of ten doctors choose), I left as the owner of a third.

Now, instead of simply writing, I jot down or dash off, I lucubrate, poeticize, novelize, composerize, calligraphize. And jiminy cricket if the mark of my pen still doesn't look like the scratch of a hen.

~ March 20, 2005

· · · · ·

Lazar Palnick doesn't carry his fountain pens in his shirt pocket.

He wears them.

"If I wear a brown suit, I wear a brown pen or gold. Silver cuff links, silver pens," he says. "It's an accessory."

Mr. Palnick, a lawyer who grew up in Little Rock and is the son of the late Rabbi Elijah Ezekiel Palnick, is a fountain pen aficionado who buys new pens for important events, such as the last four presidential elections for which he served on Pennsylvania's electoral college. (Mr. Palnick has lived in Pittsburgh for nearly two decades.)

Each election since 1992, his wife, Susanne Gollin, has ordered a new pen from the Vanness Pen Shop.

"I was always in love with fountain pens as a kid," he said in a telephone interview. "But I always had cheap ones. When I started practicing law, every time I would win or settle a big case, I would go over to Vanness and get a new pen."

In Little Rock, where Mr. Palnick worked as a civil rights lawyer with John Walker, he signed the 1989 Pulaski County schools desegregation settlement with a fountain pen.

He owns about one-hundred-twenty pens of many vintages. Most of his pens cost three-hundred dollars to six-hundred dollars, the minimum, he says, for a fine pen. He frequents flea markets and estate sales, where he has bought valuable old pens for as little as fifteen bucks.

"I like the flow of the ink," he says, "playing with all of the gadgets — inkwells, blotters, cartridges. ... How it feels when you write. The beauty of the pen, the intricacies of the pen ... of fancy nibs. The whole ceremony that goes with filling up your pen."

The fountain pen lends a traditional air to other traditions; at the electoral college, electors cast their ballots in a ballot box that dates to the election of George Washington.

"Two of the pens my wife bought me actually elected the president of the United States," he says.

Although Mr. Palnick has bought pens in big cities, Vanness is his favorite shop. "When I want a new pen," he says, "I always call Vanness first."

Vanness sells fountain pens by companies from Cross and Parker to Sheaffer, Conklin and Waterman. Lawyers, accountants, doctors, EMTs and newspaper reporters buy fountain pens, which start in the twenty-five dollar range and go as high as you want. Vanness recently sold a one-thousand six-hundred-eighteen dollar Divine Proportion pen by Visconti, an Italian maker.

Mont Blanc, one of the most famous makers of high-dollar pens, isn't one of Mr. Palnick's favorites. He owns two, but didn't buy either.

He obtained one at a Little Rock clothes-cleaning establishment, where he thought he had left a pen in a suit. The clerk pulled out a pen — a 1950s piston-filled Mont Blanc — that wasn't his and gave it to him with the caveat that he would call if the owner ever tried to claim it.

"My pen was back at the house," he says.

He has lost one: A pickpocket relieved him of it in New York as he headed for a celebration the night the Democrats nominated Bill Clinton as their presidential candidate.

The trick to keeping a fountain pen is to uncap it when someone borrows it.

"They will come find you to give it back," he says. "There will be ink all over them. I never lose a pen."

~ June 11, 2006

• • • • •

I lost Daddy's gray Esterbrook the other day.
I knew I should have quit carrying it.

For a while after I chipped the cap, in fact, I did leave it at home in the Mason jar on my dresser.

But I liked to take notes with the same pen with which Daddy scratched out letters and paid bills at the desk that still sits in the den at my parents' house in Louisiana.

Now I have lost it, a piece of family history, a tangible connection to my father.

This Esterbrook was at least fifty years old. That's about all I know about it. Mama doesn't remember where it came from. Daddy might, but conversation with him is difficult these days, and his comprehension often evasive. If he could write, I would put a fountain pen in his left hand.

Two years ago, Mama gave me three old fountain pens from their desk: a blue Sheaffer and a green Sheaffer and the first one she relinquished, the Esterbrook.

Mike Vanness and Mike's Uncle Van at Vanness Pens refurbished the green Sheaffer and the Esterbrook, replacing the dry-rotted rubber bladders. The blue Sheaffer was beyond repair.

As a collectible, the Esterbrook is worth what I paid for it. There's the bit I chipped out of the cap, and the nib is worn to Daddy's handwriting — Mike Vanness knew just by writing with it that Daddy wrote with his left hand.

The pen is worthless, which is the case with most of the stuff I collect. The value I find in an object is knowing who has put a hand to it.

I have my grandfather's shaving brush and bowl and the seventy-five-year-old ceramic-and-iron gas space heater from my grandparents' house in El Paso.

I have in my custody the wooden napkin holder that hung in Mamadee's kitchen, and perhaps the only thing of actual value, her 1920s cornbread-stick pan, which supposedly is worth seventy-five bucks. It is not for sale. We still occasionally bake cornbread in this pan into which Mamadee herself poured cornbread batter.

The collection of my father's artifacts includes his longbow, made of lemon wood, which he bought with his half of the proceeds from the sale of a john boat his father had built.

I have two of his Ricohflex twin-lens-reflex cameras and the left-handed thirty-five-millimeter camera he bought while he was overseas for the Korean conflict.

I have at home a wooden ammo box that once served as Daddy's small portable workbench. It is blotched with spray paint and test drill holes, and when I discovered it in my parents' shed recently, it was full of obsolete and broken pipes and faucets of no earthly value. (This disease is genetic). I cleaned the box, renailed it, sanded it lightly so as not to remove Daddy's signature blotches of paint, and slathered on two cans of polyurethane. Junk. But good nostalgic junk.

Aside from the room I need to warehouse the past, my sentimentality generally is harmless. Then I do something careless like losing Daddy's pen.

I last used Daddy's Esterbrook pen halfway through the day Wednesday. Chances are it will float to the top of my messy desk in the newsroom.

If it doesn't, I will grieve for a little while, as if I have lost a finger, and pledge to be more careful, if not less sappy and sentimental.

My carelessness I might cure. Might, I said. For the sensitive among us, however, sentimentality is beyond the fix of science or the will; the loss of beloved possessions elicits the most profound and eloquent expressions of grief from the bereaved, especially if the object is a fountain pen. So here it is — my eloquent self-expression of sadness over the loss of Daddy's Esterbrook:

Aww, man!

I never found that pen. But some time later, Fernando Padilla, a Little Rock lawyer and fountain pen lover, handed me a replacement Esterbrook that was exactly like my father's. Alas, lightening struck again, this time in the shape of a burglar. In the summer of 2012, someone broke into my car on a downtown parking lot, and a glasses case was among the things he took; the case, however, contained no reading glasses — only two fountain pens: An old Sheaffer and the replacement Esterbrook. On March 1, 2014, at the annual Arkansas Pen Club show, Mr. Padilla steered me to a table where I found a second replacement Esterbrook. As of March 31, 2014, the pen remains in my possession.

· · · · ·

After I rhapsodized in a column about fountain pens. Ed Garner, a state rep from Maumelle, rhapsodized right back in a letter — written, of course, with a fountain pen, a Mont Blanc Diplomat, to be exact.

"Words set to paper with a fountain pen are purchased from the author's soul, chosen and executed with great consideration," he and his Diplomat waxed. "It is as if the method of their birth gives them kinship to words penned by great masters.

"Using a fine pen as a craft tool is a remembrance that writing is an art and words are of value.

"In politics, any time I would sign a candidate filing, it felt more important," he says. "I would not be surprised to see fountain pens come back.

"It's one of the good things we have from a time past," he says. "You tend to take care of them. I don't misplace them. ... I keep up with it like I do a watch."

· · · · ·

Sam Highsmith, a charter member of the Arkansas Pen Club, owns about three-hundred fountain pens, but he is not, he insists, a collector. He is an accumulator. The difference, he says, is that he uses his pens. He doesn't keep them back, hoping their value will increase.

His accumulation of and love for fountain pens began with four fountain pens that belonged to his grandfather, Samuel M. Casey, an attorney in Batesville from 1895 to 1945.

Sam took the pens to Orville Vanness, who "polished them, put in new sacks, polished the points," Sam says. "He charged me ten dollars for all four. Plus he gave me a bottle of Sheaffer's ink."

~ March 6, 2008

RUSSELLVILLE — The fountain pen was almost beyond repair — no clip on the cap, no nib. Just the barrel and the cap.

"You're looking at fifty dollars to repair this pen," Danny Fudge told the man from Jacksonville who asked him to restore it. "This pen isn't worth fifty dollars."

The man's answer needed no clarification.

"It was my mother's pen."

"Say no more," Danny replied.

Danny, pastor of Missionary Baptist Church here, feels the weight when someone entrusts a pen to him for repair.

"He's going to put ink in that pen and write with it, the pen his mother wrote with," Danny says. "It's a connection to the past ... a connection to where we come from."

Danny owns two pens that connect him to his past, which was a tough one. His father died from complications of diabetes when Danny was two,, and his mother died when he was ten.

As a teenager, Danny was living in Mountain View with his maternal grandparents when he discovered a box of his parents' belongings in the barn — wallets, pocketknives, marbles. And two fountain pens.

He has no memory of his father, but he owns his pen.

He last saw his mother over a closed-circuit television, where she spoke to him from her hospital bed. He can't hold her, but whenever he's of a mind to, he can hold her fountain pen.

He has owned, he reckons, eight-hundred pens, but his collection stands at about two-hundred. He has built a wooden display case, which he keeps in his office at the church.

"I'm a unique guy. If everybody's doing it, I don't want to do it," he says. "I don't like modern things. I can't see passing a keyboard down."

Like anything handed down, the nicks and scratches are what makes a thing special. When he had finished restoring the pen of the man from Jacksonville, he had only to polish it up. But he had noticed a distinguishing characteristic about the pen, so he called the man. "You don't want me to take out the bite marks on the end of the barrel, do you?"

As Danny expected, the man said no.

~ April 19, 2007

To stalk a mockingbird

Once again, I have frightened Harper Lee.

That wasn't my intention, of course. I was only trying to figure out where she wrote her perennially best-selling novel, *To Kill a Mockingbird*. (Perennially best-selling novel, by the way, now is part of the book's official title.)

My search led to New York. That was more than a year ago. Only recently, however, did I learn I had spooked her.

For the record, since this may be my only notable contribution to American literature, I have found where Harper Lee wrote her novel about Scout, Jem, Atticus, Dill and Boo Radley. Or at least I have determined the locations with as much certainty as one can, since Miss Lee won't talk to reporters, nor will her family and friends talk to reporters about Miss Lee.

My history with Miss Nelle, as she is known in her hometown of Monroeville,

Alabama, goes back to 1993 and my arrival as a columnist at the Mobile Register.

Since I had come to work in her home state, I decided I was going to be the one to land the Harper Lee interview. Never mind that literary luminaries as bright as George Plimpton, founding editor of Paris Review, had failed. (I once called Mr. Plimpton, to inquire about his efforts to speak to Miss Lee. He told me that he was certain he saw someone peeking out the curtains of her home in Monroeville when he knocked on her front door.)

My strategy was simple if not subtle: I would visit her town as often as possible, write columns about my visits, and mention her name every time. (In my six years at the newspaper, according to Debby Stearns, librarian at the Mobile Register, I mentioned Miss Nelle in ten of approximately twelve-hundred columns — so she was mentioned in point-zero-zero-five percent of them, hardly a verbal assault.)

Within my first month on the job in Mobile, I drove the two hours to Monroeville and went to the historic courthouse whose courtroom was the model for the courtroom in the movie. This was the courtroom where her father had lawyered. I rented a videotape copy of the movie from the shop across the street from the courthouse, and with the help of the keeper of the courthouse, I moved a video player into the courtroom and watched the movie. When Tom Robinson sat in the witness chair, I sat in the witness chair. When the kids sat in the balcony, I watched from the balcony. I wrote a column about it.

Another year, I was a juror in the stage version of the novel, which local actors produce in the courthouse every spring. I wrote a column about it.

Then there was the time I actually met Miss Nelle. I had been told that her favorite place for coffee was the Hardee's in Monroeville. I happened to be in the neighborhood early one Saturday, so I stopped in.

At one table I saw a man and two women, one of whom I thought might be Miss Nelle. I hung back and waited for them to finish breakfast. When they stood, the woman I thought might be the author looked nothing like you'd expect an author of such renown to look. With her purse strapped across her chest, she looked slight and almost timid, like any senior citizen who might have disembarked from a tour bus for breakfast on the way to see the leaves in New England. Or Harper Lee's house. And Hardee's? That is not where you expect a world-famous writer to hang.

I followed the trio out of the restaurant, and the woman I thought was Miss Nelle broke off from the other two, who entered a car. In the couple's car, I noticed a "clergy" placard on the driver's side of the dashboard and gambled that if the man was a preacher, there was a fifty-fifty chance he'd tell me the truth.

"Is that Harper Lee?" I asked.

"Yes," he said.

So I went to the car Miss Nelle had cranked and rapped my knuckles against her window. Much to my surprise, she rolled down the window. As I like to tell people, if someone who looks like me rapped on my car window, I'd throw her in reverse and stomp the gas. But she rolled down the window.

Then, with all the cleverness and originality I could muster, I boldly announced: "I enjoyed your book."

Then I extended my hand, which she graciously took, shook and then replied simply: "Thank you."

Knowing how she feels about reporters, I didn't tell her I was one.

A year later, true to my strategy, I wrote a column about the day I met Harper Lee.

I never heard a word from her, so I never knew whether she ever saw what I wrote about her. I never knew whether she appreciated my admiration for her and her book.

One day, I found out.

Tim Ferrell, a friend of mine, received an invitation from an aunt for a weekend of hunting near her home near Monroeville. When he arrived at his aunt's, he noticed the dining room was laid out for company, and upon his inquiry, his aunt told him that Miss Nelle and her sister Miss Alice, a sneaker-clad lawyer in her 80s who was still practicing, would be over for lunch the next day.

Tim made a quick trip downtown to buy three hardbound copies of *To Kill a Mockingbird*, one of which was for me.

After lunch the next day, Miss Nelle signed the first two of Tim's copies without fanfare. When Tim handed the third to her and told her it was for Jay Grelen, the newspaper guy, she set the book in her lap and said: "That's the man who's been stalking me."

So there was my answer, and the first evidence I'd won her attention, if not her undying adoration.

Now I was ready to move in and claim my interview.

I made another trip to Monroeville, made telephone contacts and came up with the name of Thomas Lane Butts, pastor, who, as it turns out, was the Methodist minister who had confirmed Miss Lee's identity for me that day outside Hardee's.

He was a longtime friend of Miss Nelle's, and he was not the least hesitant to talk about her. He invited me to his office in Monroeville, where offered insights about Miss Nelle, told me where she went for fried catfish and shared with me excerpts of letters she had written from New York, including one in which she bragged about the fresh beans Alabama friends had brought on a recent visit.

She never traded on her name, he said, except for once when tickets to a New York show were scarce. She pulled out a credit card at the window, Mr. Butts said, and the ticket taker recognized her name and found tickets to sell to Miss Nelle.

Miss Nelle has been called a recluse. That is not accurate. She moves about freely in Monroeville, where she winters, and apparently lives as she pleases in New York.

She simply doesn't grant interviews, and her family and friends guard her privacy. She occasionally will appear at events held in her honor. In 1998, she accepted an honorary degree at commencement exercises at Springhill College in Mobile.

She stipulated one thing: That the school was not to alert the press ahead of the event. The Mobile Register, as a newspaper should, heard about it, which nearly killed her appearance.

Glen Andrews, a *Mobile Register* photographer, took a picture of her, and she liked it so much that she sent Glen a note of thanks.

That photograph, the Reverend Mr. Butts told me, was my ticket to an interview with Nelle Harper Lee. If I delivered her a copy of the photograph, he said, he would convince her to talk to me.

So Glen made a print of his picture, which I had mounted in a Victorian oval frame. I mailed it to Monroeville with a letter, in which I poured the syrup on thick. "I understand that if ever you grant an interview, not only will that be a gift to those who will read it, it will be a gift beyond measure to the writer," I gushed.

I rang every bell, tooted every whistle. I even worked catfish into the letter, which I ended with what I considered a rather clever postscript: "I hope you have saved all the letters like mine over the years. You could publish a collection of all the hogwash you have received from reporters wanting an interview. I'll bet you've got some famous names in there, and some purple prose to beat the band. Title it, 'Dear Miss Lee' ... "

Didn't work. Not even close.

She returned the photograph with a one-page letter scolding me for intruding on her privacy and telling me that, feeling about me as she did, she couldn't keep the picture.

I replied in a brief note that she never would hear from me again, and she wrote back saying thanks, that maybe I was a swell guy after all, and that she would look forward to reading my columns.

Based on her initial response, I'd bet Boo Radley's trinkets that Miss Lee would have field-dressed the Reverend Doctor Mister Thomas Lane Butts on the front lawn of the Methodist church if she had known how freely he had spoken with me, how many personal anecdotes he had shared and that he had promised me an interview with her if I would send her that photograph.

· · · · ·

And that was the end of my pursuit of Nelle Harper Lee. But it wasn't the last time I'd disturb her.

My Harper Lee project had a second part, other than the attempt to interview her. I wanted to find the residence where she wrote the book. "One thing I really would like to do," I'd written in my letter to her, "is to see the cold-water flat where you wrote *To Kill a Mockingbird*. Like the Margaret Mitchell house in Atlanta, there would be some magic in seeing where you wrote."

For the record, and no surprise, Miss Nelle wasn't a bit of help with that idea either.

But a pleasant researcher at the New York Public Library was of great assistance. She dug out the New York telephone books from the years Miss Nelle would have been writing her book and copied for me the pages on which her telephone listing appeared.

During the years 1954 through 1961, according to the Manhattan directories, "Lee, Nelle Harper" lived on four streets: Second Avenue, Fifth Avenue, York Avenue (where she stayed the longest, at least according to the phone pages) and East 77th Avenue.

So on August 13, 2001, armed with a camera, I took the subway from Union Square to Miss Nelle's New York neighborhood.

From the outside, the five-story, fifteen-unit building at 403 East 77th Street looked like a place a novelist would live and work.

The walls of the bottom floor are stucco, and the door to the downstairs foyer had a new brass doorknob. The top four floors were red brick, with the fire escape zig-zagging down the middle as if to zipper the building shut.

Four windows opened across each floor. Air-conditioning units protruded from eight of the windows. I buzzed intercoms until a woman in an apartment answered. She had lived there a long time, she said, and had never heard of Harper Lee.

The next of Miss Nelle's homes on my list, the most posh address at 665 Fifth Avenue across from Central Park, now is the Rolex building. Whatever that is, but it's not apartments.

I made my most interesting discovery at her former residence at 1540 Second Avenue, which also looks like a place where a young woman from Alabama would live to write a best-selling novel. A restaurant occupies the bottom floor of the four-story building. The restaurant belongs to a Miss Lee.

The name of the restaurant is Nancy Lee's Pig Heaven Restaurant, a perfectly appropriate establishment to install below the former workplace of an acclaimed Southern writer who also happens to be named Lee.

This other Lee, however, isn't from Alabama. She's from China, and she had never heard of Harper Lee either.

My trip to York Avenue was both my most disappointing and the closest I came to gold. At a certain corner of York Avenue, where the apartment was supposed to be, I could not find the address I was looking for, but there was a building near the site. If the Literary Society ever puts up a plaque there, it could read: "Somewhere in this general vicinity, Nelle Harper Lee probably worked on *To Kill a Mockingbird*."

(If you ever have wondered why Miss Lee chose Harper as her professional name over Nelle, simply say her first name and last name together. Say it more quickly if you don't hear it the first time.)

I crossed the street to a take-out Italian restaurant and struck up a conversation with the proprietor, who informed me that the original building had been demol-ished. When I told him why I was interested, he smiled. Big.

"She gets coffee here every day," he said. "You missed her by three hours."

My face, I'm sure, lit up brighter than his. I flipped open my little notepad and fired off one of those incisive Harper Lee questions, right up there with my witty: "I liked your book," the day I met her.

With all the solemnity and IQ this moment demanded, I pinned the restaurateur to the wall: "Does she take her coffee black?"

His Italian face went dark. "No, no. That's all," he said, turning away from me. "I don't want to make her mad."

So I ordered sirloin lasagna and a glass of iced tea, which, of course, I had to sweeten myself. (He forgave my aggressive interviewing technique and brought me a plastic tub of sugar from the kitchen.) As I departed, I left a greeting: "Tell her Jay Grelen from Alabama says hello."

Then I walked two blocks east to a little park that overlooks the Hudson River and, while I ate, I wondered how often Miss Nelle walks this path.

At the end of my day, which was intermittently hot and rainy (and as it turns out, the last time I ever would see the Twin Towers, which came down a month later), I had accounted for all of the likeliest places where Harper Lee may have worked on her novel. Except for her house in Monroeville, but that's nothing new. Everybody knows where that is.

As pigeons skulked about hoping for a scrap of my lasagna (I wondered if that's how I look to Miss Nelle), this rather obvious observation occurred at the end of my search for the birthplace of *To Kill a Mockingbird*. Novels really aren't written in a place. They are merely put to paper in a location — an apartment, at a desk, in a city. A writer, of course, writes a novel in her mind and heart, the words streaming out of the cord of memory that connects them. The hands, on orders from above, simply transcribe the stories with whatever mechanical devices are available — a Big Chief tablet and a fountain pen, or a ream of paper and a typewriter. I had complicated the matter. To see the birthplace of *To Kill a Mockingbird*, I need only have looked at a picture of Nelle Harper Lee.

And that was that. I took the subway back to Union Square, picked up my luggage, caught a taxi to LaGuardia airport and left New York, with no notion that within twenty-four hours, word of my visit would reach Miss Nelle and disturb her peace.

It was more than a year later, however, that I heard from one of her friends that Miss Nelle "got word that someone had been snooping around after her in New York and was a bit frightened about it."

So that is how, for a second time, I spooked the author of one of the best-read and most influential American books ever written.

Not to fear, Miss Nelle. It was only that skulking newspaper man from Mobile. And if you haven't sampled it, may I suggest the Italian deli's sirloin lasagna. With, of course, sweet tea.

You talk. I'll buy.

This story has appeared in various forms in The Sun News *of Myrtle Beach, South Carolina, the* Mobile Register *and the* Arkansas Democrat-Gazette.

For a long time, Kathy Davison has been joking with friends that some day her sweet tea would win a prize.

And now it has.

On the Fourth of July 2007, a panel of eight judges proclaimed Kathy's the best of the bunch.

She was one of six tea makers to put reputation and emotions on the line in the Sixth Ever Southern Sweet Tea Sipoff. (We can't say sixth annual because there has been a nine-year stretch since the last one.)

The secret to her sweet tea, says the newly crowned Sweet Tea Champion, is in the steeping and the love.

"I love it," she says.

The other Sweet Tea makers who competed were:

Marilyn Lane Lee, Alexander; Fredda Lackey, Little Rock; Lesa Pettit, Little Rock; Lois Smith, Little Rock; and Samme Wallace, Benton.

The number was small, but the six tea makers brewed plenty of tea for the brave panel of judges: Joy Buffalo; Bobby Fuller; Carolyn Fuller; Frank Lockwood; Rex Nelson; Brad Turner; Mike Tyler; and Robin Ward.

The terrific music, provided by the Sweet Tea String Society, included "Pig Ankle Rag," which they played for the Baby Bottle Sipoff.

(The STSS is Jonathan Trawick, guitar, and Austin DuVall, Tim Trawick and Josh Turner, fiddle.)

Contestant Lois Mae Smith, according to her daughter Margaret, makes five to six gallons of sweet tea at least twice a week. "More when needed."

The tea making is ceremonial.

"When she makes it," Margaret reports, "she evenly distributes the hot tea over each pitcher that contains just the right amount of sugar. Nothing fancy here, just plain sweet tea."

Until our new Sweet Tea Champ settled in Beebe eight years ago, she had been an Army brat, both as a child and an adult. She has spread the gospel of Sweet Tea in twenty-two states.

Her love of tea came, she says, with her first encounter. Her family had traveled into the Southern region and stopped at a restaurant.

"They asked if we wanted it sweet or unsweet," she recalls. "I thought, 'Wait a minute. You pre-sweeten the tea? I knew I needed to move to the South.'"

• • • • •

Last year, after Frank Lockwood had signed the contract to judge in the Southern Sweet Tea Sip-Off, he asked a question that raised serious doubt about his qualifications:

"What," he asked, "are we going to cleanse our palate with?"

Cleanse our palate?

Now Frank is a man who is comfortable in his manhood, but what kind of a manly man would ask a question like that?

His question forces us to another issue of some importance. To wit: Do Southerners even have palates?

Taste buds, we know about but palates? Of all the body parts Mama taught me to wash behind, between and under, she never once told me to clean my palate, much less cleanse it.

Frank, the *Arkansas Democrat-Gazette*'s religion editor, isn't a Southerner and very well may have a palate, but we can't know for sure because the editors have not instituted random tests for palates. Just so he'll be comfortable, though, I'll set an old toothbrush and the Bon Ami at his spot.

• • • • •

Saphronia Necessary's sweet tea is famous now, but her recipe stays in the family.

"The only secret I'll let out is it's got Lipton's in it," says Brandy Harper, her granddaughter and this year's Sweet Tea champ.

Mrs. Necessary pretty much raised Brandy, who dedicated her victory to her grandmother. Mrs. Necessary died May 13 at the age of ninety-one.

"I'm the only one in the family who makes Mamaw's tea," Brandy said after seven judges picked her tea as the best of the thirteen batches they tasted.

Wendy Gregan took second, Lannece Mayo, third, and Tanya Clement and Denise Nesbitt tied for fourth.

The other entrants were Betty Jo Adams, Tina Boyles, Kim and Ellen Schreyer, Pat Kimbrell, Marilyn Lane Lee, Susie Marsh and Lesa Pettit.

While thirteen brave souls put their tea on the line, eleven people demonstrated great courage by drinking sweet tea from a baby bottle. In public.

Craig O'Neill, that famous news guy from KTHV, was our surprise celebrity contestant. He looked perfectly natural nursing a five-ounce baby bottle.

Evan Nesbitt was the first to finish. Josie Lee, only five years old, wins for bravery. She was the youngest contestant by ten years. The others were: Bridget Mendenhall; Adrienne Scoggin; Lydia Mayo; Benjamin Mayo; Gerald Mayo; John Gregan; Katie Pate; and Wesley Pate. (The Pate siblings recently moved here from Alabama. Their father is a minister at Geyer Springs Baptist Church.)

The judges were Joy "Wash Your Hands" Buffalo; Frankie "Sweet'n'Low" Clay (You've seen him making pancakes on TV. He's available. Call his agent.); Frank Lockwood, *Democrat-Gazette* religion editor; the indefatigable wife-husband team of Melissa and Rex Nelson; Randy Pate, the aforementioned minister; and David Tackett, co-owner of MorningSide Bagels on Maumelle Boulevard. (Out of concern for Frank Lockwood's purported palate, David provided bagel chips as palate cleansers. Bonafide New York-style bagels — they boil them before they bake them. New York bagels and sweet tea under the same tent. Jay-Bob is multicultural.)

Bob Buffalo, husband of the hand-washing woman, kept the Sip-Off on the rails. Roxane Tackett, David's wife and partner in bagels, and their daughter, Jennifer, poured tea for the judges. Austin and Evan Nelson, brothers and math wizards and the sons of Rex and Melissa, discarded the samples and tallied the scores.

Mike Vanness of Vanness Pen Shop (subliminal message: You need a fountain pen.) engraved the pewter pitcher.

Tim Trawick, Arkansas' 2007 fiddle champion, his son Jonathan and their friend "Mandolin Bill" Nesbitt, provided the bluegrass.

As for our new Sweet Tea champ, Miss Saphronia's granddaughter has been making tea since she was five.

"I squeezed the tea bags and put them in the trash," she says. "I stirred the sugar. I stood on this special stool — Mamaw called it my kitchen stool. My son uses it now. He's next in line to get the recipe."

~ July 5, 2008

say her name, the birds stop their singing

Her name is a mouthful, a bell-ringer, a blue-ribbon one-line poem, a song in nine syllables. A twenty-one-letter novel in three words. An ode to all that is Southern and beautiful.

She should have been a star in the stories of a Southern writer like Eudora Welty.

Her first name is an autumn wind whispering through cedar boughs. Her three names spoken together are violins and cello emoting Pachelbel's Canon in D.

Saphronia.

Saphronia May.

Saphronia. May. Necessary.

Saphronia was born an Elwell in Stuttgart in 1916, in a time that the name was popular, though this Saphronia was named for her grandmothers, not for style.

Her father was a railroad man, her mother a stay-at-home. But not always strictly stay at home. For reasons unknown, says Merle Necessary Webb, Saphronia's mother left her husband and moved back in with her mother. She would leave Saphronia May and Ida Fay home alone for days at a time in their house beside the tracks.

"My grandmother would leave them with biscuits and onions," says Merle, Saphronia's youngest daughter. "My mother was five, and my aunt was three."

When Saphronia started school, young Ida Fay would spend the day in back of the classroom.

"The Mexican woman next door had a fire in the backyard and a flat iron," Merle says. "She made tortillas and put beans on them. If it weren't for those tortillas and beans, some days they wouldn't eat."

In time, Saphronia's mother remarried, and in 1931, the family relocated to Hot Springs, where she opened the Broadway Cafe.

"Mother worked there before she went to school and after she got home from school. She still took care of Aunt Fay, and my grandmother didn't . ... Mother wanted to go to nursing school, but her mother wanted her in the restaurant.

"So, when I decided to go to nursing school, mother did everything she could to help."

That, Merle says, sums up Saphronia.

In 1937, Saphronia married a Necessary from Virginia. Eventually, they settled in Hot Springs and produced four offspring: Jim. Nancy. Robert. Merle.

Jim was born in the apartment above the restaurant where they lived.

"[Nancy] was mentally retarded and handicapped," Merle says. "My mother devoted her life to her."

Even when Saphronia was in her eighties, and her children made her put Nancy in a nursing home, she saw Nancy every day.

In the early days, Saphronia worked at a shirt factory. Then she managed the hat department at the Kmart. She was a founding member of the Melting Pot Genea-logical Society of Hot Springs.

Saphronia May Necessary died peacefully at her home in Hot Springs in May 2008 at the age of ninety-one with Merle and Goldie the cat at her side.

· · · · ·

Saphronia made her tea in a stainless steel pitcher stamped with "U.S. Marine Corps," which a great uncle brought home from service.

Sometimes, still, Brandy the Sweet Tea Champ will mix a batch of tea in that pitcher. The one that belonged to Saphronia May Necessary, who, Brandy and Merle say, is the real champ.

~ **July 2008**

Dr. Peter Bost: 'A deathly scourge'

Roger Bost remembers the swooshing cadence of an iron lung, steady as a clock: One breath every three seconds. Twenty per minute.

The urgent cadence of life for those flattened by polio. An insistent rhythm for Mr. Bost, a young Arkansas doctor who was serving his residency at Duke Hospital in North Carolina.

Dr. Bost, a young man no longer, recalls clearly: Kind of an eerie sound.

The doctor, eighty-eight now, lives a quiet life with Kathryn Bost, his wife of sixty-six years, in a home on the side of a hill where seven antique clocks count off the seconds in clock-tocks muffled and steady.

Dr. Bost well remembers the iron lungs, and in the quiet of his home, one of the doctors who helped to slay the virus, quietly imitates the iron lung: Swoosh in. Pause. Swoosh out.

You could hear them a fair distance away, he says. All day long.

Summertime, before Salk and Sabin, was the scariest season. Community swimming pools, packed with kids who cared little for hygiene, were Olympic-size polio-breeding Petri dishes. The virus raced kid to kid, surviving hand to mouth.

"It was a deathly scourge," says the doctor, who helped obliterate the scourge in his home state and later in a state far from his home.

In North Carolina in 1948, the epidemic was so severe that Duke Hospital filled its pediatric ward with iron lungs and closed it to all but polio patients.

Late one night, Dr. Bost tapped the spine of a sick two-year-old and rushed to the lab with a pipette filled with the boy's spinal fluid. Because of the hour, no one was on duty in the lab to take the sample and test it. So he would test it himself. He put the pipette to his lips to blow it into an empty test tube.

But: "I was tired."

Twenty-hours-without-a-break tired.

"I sucked the fluid into my mouth."

He scrubbed out his mouth with the bitter tincture of green soap. The tests confirmed polio. Which meant he had sucked the polio virus into his mouth.

"While I was in the lab," he says, "that child died."

The virus didn't infect Dr. Bost.

In 1964, Dr. Bost, by then a pediatrician in Fort Smith, was chairman of the polio committee of the Arkansas Medical Society, which organized and deployed the state's mass distribution of sugar cubes infused with the Sabin vaccine. The nationwide campaign virtually eradicated polio.

Dr. Bost's experience led to a request for his help in Cochabamba, Bolivia, a polio-stricken city of 200,000 souls and fewer than 200 indoor toilets.

Dr. Bost and Little Rock anesthesiologist Dr. Wayne Glenn delivered iron lungs and a million doses of the Sabin vaccine.

The doctors rushed by ambulance from the airport to the hospital to treat a polio-stricken child. "We had that child on a respirator within thirty minutes," he says.

In Bolivia, too, the campaign succeeded.

All these years later, Dr. Bost remembers the details. And in his hillside home, the cadence of his seven clocks, steady as an iron lung, is inescapable. Tock. Pause. Tock.

~ July 18, 2010

Dr. Roger Bost died November 19, 2013.

Hi Ho Steve-O fought polio

Not everything that Steve Stephens does shows up in the newspaper or on television.

A search of *Arkansas Democrat–Gazette* archives for "Steve Stephens" and "polio," for instance, yields nothing.

But let history show that Steve Stephens answered the call, literally, that led to the virtual eradication of polio in a city in Bolivia.

To Arkansas teenagers in the late 1950s and early '60s, Steve was "Hi Ho Steve-O," host of "Steve's Show," a dance-party TV show.

KTHV-TV broadcast the half-hour show six days a week. In 1964, Steve-O, a Marine and a veteran of the Korean war, created "Eye on Arkansas," a noontime show that publicized the entertainers who performed at the Vapors nightclub in Hot Springs.

The stars who appeared on Steve-O's show, according to the biography the late Chuck Cunning wrote about him, included Liberace, the Smothers Brothers and

Brother Dave Gardner.

Steve has worked in public relations, travel and government. As chairman of the Partners of the Americas program in Arkansas, he met with the presidents of Bolivia, Peru and Costa Rica.

In 1971, Steve's counterpart in Maine contacted him to say that the Bolivian chapter of Partners had contacted him by shortwave radio to ask for help for the city of Cochabamba. Polio was raging in the city that was home to two-hundred-thousand people and fewer than two-hundred indoor toilets.

Steve-O went to work, calling doctors and counterparts around the country. The chancellor of the University of Arkansas Medical Center offered to send a million doses of polio vaccine and recommended a Little Rock pediatrician for the mission.

Three days later, a Braniff Airlines jet, which the airline donated for the humanitarian mission at Steve's request, was bound for Bolivia carrying nothing but medicine, iron lungs, respirators, suction machines and two Arkansas doctors — Roger Bost, the pediatrician, and Wayne Glenn, an anesthesiologist.

Steve Stephens talks about the mission in heroic terms that Dr. Bost won't: "These doctors and a host of volunteers along the way were able to stop a polio epidemic in a Bolivian city with a strange name, saving countless lives of people they didn't even know existed. A grateful city awarded both men honorary doctorates at the University of Cochabamba, and to this day they are regarded as the saviors of the city."

• • • • •

When Hi Ho Steve-O started his broadcast career on KNBY radio in his hometown of Newport, his name was Rufus James Stephens.

At the suggestion of KTHV program director Jack Bomar, who hired Rufus James at the television station, he changed his first name to Steve and eventually took his father's name, Owen, as his middle name. So Rufus James became Stephen Owen Stephens with initials befitting a fellow who likes to make the occasional rescue.

~ July 20, 2010

Forever Juanita

Bill handed the photographs to me one at a time: Juanita when she was sixteen.

I laid it near the edge of his wooden desk, its shine worn dull by a forest of paper pushed across it over the decades, a desktop big enough for full-court basketball.

Juanita when she was seventeen.

I laid it to the right of the first. Juanita when she was eighteen. Juanita fourteen years ago.

"We probably got the only marriage license issued in the country on Christmas Eve that year," Bill says.

They married on Christmas Eve, the year before we dropped the atomic bomb. This love commenced late in the summer of 1942. Bill had just finished throwing his paper route when he first saw Juanita, who was about to cross the street to the little windmill cafe built at Fourth and High.

When school commenced days later, he sat next to the new girl.

Their first official date was March 23, 1943. Neither ever dated another.

In the fall of 1944, Bill dropped out of the eleventh grade and followed an uncle to a construction site at Oak Ridge, Tennessee, which we now know was a significant part of the atomic-bomb project.

Bill, who was sixteen, distributed blueprints but knew none of the secrets. He knew only this: He missed Juanita.

He already had given her an engagement ring and in a letter he asked her to marry him at Christmas.

"This is so sudden," Juanita wrote back. "I'll have to think about it."

In the next sentence, Juanita wrote: "Yes. Yes."

On December 23, 1944, Bill, Juanita, her parents, Bill's mother and his future stepfather stopped at the first marriage parlor they saw in Benton.

How old are you? the justice of the peace asked.

Sixteen, Bill answered. (Juanita was seventeen.)

I can't marry you, the JP said. *If you had told me you were twenty-one, I wouldn't have questioned you.*

The next day, Christmas Eve, a Sunday, they all drove to Searcy where, with the help of Bill's future stepgranddad, they secured a marriage license at the courthouse.

Down the street, the members of a Baptist church were dedicating a new sanctuary. Bill's future stepgranddad interrupted the ceremony, spoke to the pastor, motioned the kids up, and the minister married them.

Juanita was beautiful, Bill says, beautiful in every way a person can be. She was only seventy when she died in 1997.

Bill told me this story when I stopped by his office late Christmas Eve on what would have been their sixty-fourth anniversary. An hour later, as I put the really short version of this love story to paper for the Christmas Day issue, the whole thing played back for me like a clip from a black-and-white Christmas movie:.

On Christmas Eve, I walk into a big room in the basement of the newspaper building where every desk and office is empty except one, and there's Bill, alone, small, and he shares his true tale of love everlasting, the older man honoring the younger with the gift of this story of romance. When he tears up yet again, the older man effects a gruff voice and gently pounds his desk to distract from the red eyes.

"You give me my pictures back," he says, and from the church across the street the Christmas Eve bells chime the time.

He pulls the second picture out again. "She was always seventeen."

~ **December 25, 2008**

My mama's hot chocolate

It happened every Christmas. When I lived in Mobile, Alabama. In Oklahoma City. Ditto Myrtle Beach, South Carolina. And now in Arkansas.

I would publish my mother's hot chocolate recipe with the suggestion that readers store it in a safe place, and before the ink had dried on the newsprint, someone was writing to request that I reprint the recipe because he – by whom I mean Ed Bibb – had lost it.

"I saved the recipe," he wrote, "but somehow it was lost."

The recipe seekers always were polite and apologetic. Sandy Bakke wrote: "I thought I'd put the recipe ... in a safe place. The place may be safe, but I've forgotten where! ... Of course, I'll need to bring some to school once all know I've the recipe again — that's what happened when I made my mother's recipe for zucchini bread."

Maureen Johnson's request for a reprint wrenched the heart. "I had your recipe on my fridge for months, and last week I went to Kroger to get the ingredients. I bought them, but in leaving the store, I lost my folder that had my list and your recipe in it!

"I went back to the store, and some employees even looked for it. I looked in the parking lot under cars ... .

"The reason I wanted to make the recipe is my mom lives with us, and, with the weather getting colder, she gets cold. And that's due to the medicines she takes. She just turned ninety. She loves hot chocolate, and the store-bought stuff is really so-so.

"I'll be forever grateful, and mom will have a warm tummy."

I, of course, complied, but that wasn't enough for Maureen, who was a repeat offender. She lost the recipe a second time, and in her second request for mercy, she told me more about her mother, Ingeborg Junius, who was born in Ulzen, Germany, in 1915; moved to Chicago in 1927; and worked as a waitress at the Northshore Country Club in Chicago until she was eighty-five. At ninety-five, she was drinking Granny Grelen's Hot Chocolate in Arkansas.

Those who didn't lose it liked to brag. One afternoon at the grocery store in Edmond, Oklahoma, a woman stuck her face in front of mine and demanded: "Are you Grelen?"

I was too surprised to lie. Then she showed me her copy of the hot chocolate column, which she had clipped and brought along as a shopping list.

Delmer Tew was one of the first losers after I printed the recipe in the *Mobile Register* in the 1990s. He tracked me down in Arkansas from Flomaton, Alabama, to assure me he still has the recipe. Delmer, who gives Ziploc-bagsful of the mix as a Christmas gift to members of the choir at First Baptist in Century, Florida, where he is minister of music, carries the recipe in his wallet. "It's the copy I wrote down the day I called and you read it to me on the telephone," he said. "When I go to the Piggly Wiggly, I stock up."

Now you, too, can mix it up in your very own home. No power tools or special equipment required. Mama isn't sure where she found the recipe, but she has been mixing it up for more than twenty years. My daughters, Samantha and Rebekah, call my mother Granny, and since we haven't found the origin of the recipe, I call it Granny Grelen's Hot Chocolate Mix.

Mama recommends Mason jars filled with the mix and tied with a red ribbon as a Christmas gift.

Find a big (at least two-gallon) plastic container with a tight lid – Delmer uses an aluminum pot — and pour in:

One eight-quart box of powdered milk (The brand names work best.)

One one-and-a-half pound or two pound box of instant chocolate drink (such as Nesquik; my daughters like the Kroger brand)

One twelve-ounce jar of powdered creamer (Coffeemate, et cetera; Delmer prefers Cremora.) Nonfat works well.

One one-pound box of powdered sugar

Shake it up

("I tape the edges of the lid," Delmer says, "then shake the fire out of it.")

Fill a mug a fourth to a third deep with the mix, add water that's not-quite boiling and stir. Marshmallows optional.

Baby Jesus cost twenty-nine cents.

So, too, Mary, an angel and the shepherd who is filling in for Joseph, who apparently sneaked out with the wrapping-paper scraps one Christmas.

The unblemished lamb in the manger scene sold for fifteen pieces of copper.

All painted by hand in Italy (according to the stamp on the bottom of the figures) and imported to Elmore's 5¢ and 10¢ Stores in Brewton, Alabama. That's where Mama bought the nativity set in December 1958 and where, a couple of years later, a raggedy Santa scared me to tears.

Forty-nine years later, the price tags survive on seven of the twelve figures. The humans stand on flat pedestals that are a quarter-inch-thick. The lamb stands on its own four feet, its fifteen-cent price tag still clinging to its belly.

For half a century now, Mama has erected the manger on the lamp table her parents bought for her and Daddy in Pensacola, Florida, down the road from Brewton.

The table is a two-story outfit, its top shelf half as wide as the bottom and forming the roof of the manger.

For the manger's floor, Mama now spreads glittery cotton, but back when, my kid sisters and I carpeted it with pine straw from the yard.

To the best of Mama's recollection, if she's ever missed a Christmas setting up the Nativity, it was 1977, the last Christmas she spent with her father, who lay dying in a west Texas hospital.

The nativity has become invisible with familiarity, as much a part of life at Mama's as the peanut butter cookies and chocolate chip cookies in the ancient tins in her corner kitchen cabinet. (I always check as soon as I'm in the door.)

This Christmas, for the first time in a long time, I really saw the nativity.

Late last Wednesday, after six hours over the river and through the wood and the milk-thick smoke of pine straw afire in country ditches — I sat on the cushioned chair next to the table and absorbed the nativity. Examined each figure. I brushed Baby Jesus across my right cheek. I was surprised to find that the figures were plastic. If you had asked before last week, I would have told you they were ceramic.

To hold the plastic Mary and the Christ child was to hold time in my hands, time recalled and frozen for close examination, these simple icons of our faith, tokens of promise that tightly stitch each year, each generation, to the next.

The next evening, we exchanged gifts in Mama and Daddy's living room, and the thought struck me that my teenager daughters were celebrating Christmas near the spot where the six-year-old flat-top me found my Superman suit. I had sat right there, thrilled to read the bright yellow words on the tail of the blue shirt: "Remember, this suit cannot make you fly. Only Superman can fly." I had sat there, secure, and though I didn't *know* I knew this, in my marrow I knew that I was as safe as an earthling boy.

The time has flown since my Superman days, and now I know what I had then and still have, that sense of continuity and a sense of security — my parents at one end of time, my children at the other, the priceless twenty-nine-cent Christ child watching all the time from that little maple pine-straw-covered table. My parents' lives assure me that we can make it, my daughters assure me that we will. That's a heap of grace and hope, not to mention the memories, for two bucks and ninety-two cents.

~ **December 25, 2007**

December 18, 1957: Three months after the Little Rock Nine enrolled at Central High, from the *Arkansas Democrat*: "Minnie Jean Brown, one of the nine Negro students attending Central High School, was suspended indefinitely yesterday for dumping her food on two white boys. ...

"The incident was described by [Superintendent Virgil T.] Blossom [in part] this way:

" '... The colored student lost her temper and dumped her food on the boys.' "

February 3, 1958: "Minnijean Brown, negro student at Central High School, was suspended for two weeks yesterday by Superintendent Virgil T. Blossom, who also said he would recommend to the School Board that the 16-year-old junior be expelled. ...

"Minnijean has been involved in numerous incidents with white students, the latest of which resulted in a three-day suspension. ... In that incident, Minnijean allegedly called Frankie Ann Gregg 'petty white trash' and was in turn hit by the Gregg girl's purse. Frankie Ann voluntarily withdrew from Central. ...

"If expelled, Minnijean would not be eligible for admission to any other Little Rock public school. ... By agreement with other school boards of the state, she would not be eligible to enroll in any other public school of Arkansas. ...

"In a letter to the girl's parents, Blossom said Minnijean had violated an agreement under which she had been reinstated from suspension imposed after a soup-dumping incident.

"Blossom said ... she agreed not to 'retaliate either verbally or physically to any harassment by other [white] students but to leave such thing entirely up to school authorities to handle. ...'"

February 18, 1958: "A Negro girl was expelled yesterday from Little Rock Central High School. ... Minnijean Brown was expelled ... after a 40-minute closed hearing."

February 19, 1958: "Minnie Jean Brown, Negro student permanently suspended from Central High School ... plans to begin classes Monday in the [integrated private] New Lincoln School, New York City. ...

"In confirming a report that Minnie Jean will accept a $1,050 scholarship ..., [her mother] said that 'while I'm grateful, I'm not happy that our daughter must go away at this time to attend school. ... I am not happy that children of both races are being hurt by selfish and hateful men.'"

February 22, 1958: "A bomb scare on a plane carrying Minnijean Brown ... to New York delayed departure of a morning flight. ... No bomb was found."

"Minnijean ... said that she would 'definitely be back next year to re-enter school here.'"

June 5, 1959: "NEW YORK (AP) — Minnijean Brown graduates from high school today, completing an education that was interrupted in her home town of Little Rock."

August 31, 2005: *State and city officials unveiled bronze statues of the Little Rock Nine, including a life-size likeness of Minnijean Brown Trickey, who left Little Rock yesterday and lived in Canada for more than thirty years. After the event on the north side of the capitol, the U.S. Postal Service unveiled a postage stamp in honor of the Nine. The ceremony was held at Central High School. Minnijean was there. By invitation.*

~ August 28, 2005

Minnijean: 'It's been assumed we didn't notice'

Minnijean Brown Trickey utters her feelings with undisguised impatience.

"I am," she says, "more than the chili."

Impatience unbridled, kindled in the kiln of segregation. "It's been fifty years," she says. "We can't keep talking about [chili]. It's a way of deflecting ... the complexity of the Central High crisis."

Except for her arrival at Central, Minnijean is most known for spilling chili on two white students at their lunch table in December 1957.

The school board suspended her and two months later expelled her for calling a classmate "white trash." Minnijean graduated from an integrated private school in

New York in 1959.

She majored in journalism at Southern Illinois University. In 1967, she married Roy Trickey, the son of a white Presbyterian minister, and they moved to Canada to dodge the draft.

After raising six children, she earned her bachelor's and master's degrees in social work. Divorced now, she lives with her mother in Little Rock. One daughter, Spirit, is a park ranger at the Little Rock Central High School National Historic Site.

Minnijean has devoted her life to the gospel of nonviolence. The chili drop, she says, was consistent.

She could have ignored the taunts that day, she conceded to historian Elizabeth Jacoway in an interview published in *The Arkansas Historical Quarterly* (Spring 2005). She chose instead, she says, a silent, nonviolent response. "I dropped the chili. I didn't dump a bowl of chili. I dropped the tray, the bun, the milk, the fork, the straw ... . I just opened my hands ... ."

Hers was an impatience fertilized by the hurt of jeers and taunts, of anger beyond her comprehension.

"I have been described as tough," she says of the half year she endured at Central. "If I had been, I wouldn't have been hurt so much. I was more embarrassed than mad ... not really understanding why I was feeling embarrassed. ... My life in a way is a response to growing up in a Jim Crow segregated South."

Her first awareness of "whiteness" came at the Fair Park pool. "All I could do was walk by that pool ... . Whiteness seemed to be having fun. I couldn't go in there. In the Jim Crow South, it's been assumed we didn't notice."

~ August 30, 2005

Minnijean's chili, his shirt

For nearly fifty years after Minnijean Brown Trickey dropped her lunch on Dent Gitchell in the Central High cafeteria, he remained pretty much unnoticed. Which was his preference.

In the spring 2005 issue of The Arkansas Historical Quarterly, however, historian Elizabeth Jacoway included his name in an article about Minnijean, which is what led me to call him. Until last week when we talked by phone, Dent never had spoken publicly about the moment he looked down and saw Minnijean's chili on his shirt.

In her interview with Elizabeth Jacoway, Minnijean said that Dent wasn't taunting her that day. She just happened to be standing over him when she hit her limit.

As for Dent, the incident didn't affect him: "I put a clean shirt on and went on about my business."

The year of "unbridled hatred and bigotry" at Central High, however, did go on. The student body at Central, Dent says, fell into roughly four categories:

The segs, who were the "active harassers."
Those who didn't openly harass the Nine but joined the jeering;
Those who were "just trying to be high school kids."
The fourth group, he says, was "a very, very few people who were brave enough to try to be friends with the black students."
"I'm not proud to say," Dent says, "that I was not one of them."

• • • • •

On that day in the lunchroom, Dent was vaguely aware that someone was behind him. "Normally at lunch, there was a certain amount of jeering when [the black students] walked through. I don't remember anything unusual ... until I felt something hit my head," he says. "I looked down, and there was chili running down my shirt. There was an immediate ... pandemonium."

He and Rob Pittard, a friend sitting next to him, went to the office. "I didn't want a confrontation," says Dent, a retired lawyer and law professor. "The last thing I wanted was to be identified as a 'seg.' I knew people would think I had provoked her."

Minnijean and the boys arrived at the office at the same time. The boys went home for clean clothes. Minnijean went home, too: She was suspended.

Reporters pestered Dent for an interview, but he and Rob stuck to their pact of silence.

"It's not something I'm either ashamed or proud of," he says. "It's just something that happened. ... As far as I know, my name never appeared in the press."

The encounter with Minnijean was the least memorable of the incidents he witnessed. He recalls the time during physical education class when someone drew blood with a rock to the back of Terrence Roberts' head. The coach rounded up the students and said, "kind of with a smirk on his face, 'Now you boys shouldn't do that.'"

"Witnessing things like that, seeing black students walk down the hall followed by eight or ten students hollering, calling them names. ... It changed my outlook on everything.

"The Nine were absolutely stoic. I don't know how a kid that age could have done what they did. I'd've blown my stack."

~ September 1, 2005

In March 2014, I contacted the student who was sitting next to Dent that day and accompanied Dent to the principal's office. He recalls the events clearly, he told me, and he thinks he took more of Minnijean's chili than Dent did. He has never spoken publicly about the incident and, he says, he never will. "Sleeping dogs ...," he said. He asked that I not publish his name.

Minnijean's Spirit

Little Rock Nine or not, Minnijean Brown Trickey was no icon to her daughter, Spirit Trickey.

Minnijean was Spirit's mother. Simple as that.

Spirit apprehended her mother's importance in stages.

Spirit had heard the Central High stories all her life, most often in school discussions about civil rights, usually during Black History Month.

She knew that her mother was one of many black students who volunteered to attend Central. "She wanted to walk to school," Spirit says.

When Spirit and her family attended the official opening of the Little Rock Central High School National Historic Site in 1997 and met President Clinton, Spirit sensed something of the heft of her mother's legacy.

And there was the poignant moment for Spirit in 2003 when she watched from the audience as her mother took the stage at Central High School. "In 1957," Ms. Trickey told students, "I wasn't allowed on this stage."

But that wasn't Spirit's enlightening.

· · · · ·

Spirit, who was born in Canada, moved to Little Rock in 2001. She is a National Parks ranger at the Central High museum, which is in the Mobil gas station across the street from Central High School. Now Spirit spends her days telling people from all over the place about her mother.

At the restored Mobil station where Spirit works, you can watch old film of Minnijean and the other eight as they disembark from a station wagon under guard of members of the 101st Airborne. You can cross the street and walk up the same steps where they walked amid the taunts and jeers from their new classmates. Inside the school lobby, you can see the plaque with Minnijean's name and picture.

Spirit spends her days talking about her mother and interpreting the photographs: White students hanging a black person in effigy. The hate on the faces of the students who are surrounding the Nine. Spirit watches the old film, hears Elizabeth Eckford speak tearfully of the students who slammed her into lockers.

Spirit only tells visitors that she is the daughter of one of the Nine when she thinks the information will enhance the tour. That real-life connection, she thinks, helps school children better comprehend the story.

Once in a while, Spirit will meet someone who knew her mother during that time. And time has not, Spirit notes, diminished her mother's passion for human rights. The Minnijean in those old photographs is the same Minnijean who raised her.

· · · · ·

Spirit's appreciation of her mother had nothing to do with old news reels or newspaper photographs or meeting the president of the United States. That moment came in 1996 in an appearance that clearly bespoke her mother's significance. Spirit was about sixteen at the time. She remembers her sister calling from Toronto to marvel at it, and she laughs at the memory.

This, she says, is the moment they knew their mother truly was important: "When she got on Oprah."

Minnijean's protector

That morning in September 1957, Herman Wendell Van Patten was doing what he knew was the polite and right thing to do.

In those tense times, however, with the whole country watching Little Rock attempt to desegregate, such courtesies weren't allowed. Don't do that again, his superiors in the United States Army ordered.

Mr. Van Patten, a National Guardsman federalized by President Eisenhower, had one job: Protect the Little Rock Nine. Protect them. Period. Even the slightest kindness could be an opening for trouble.

"'Always keep your eyes peeled,'" Roger Vaughan recalls the bosses telling Herman. "The colonel who talked to us told us how important it was to protect those kids. If you see a rock coming, stick your head in front of it."

In other words, protect their lives, just don't be nice to them while you are at it.

Mr. Van Patten was one of six National Guardsmen from Searcy who occupied the Jeeps front and back of the well-photographed station wagon that delivered the students to school every day.

"All of us drove some," Mr. Vaughan says. "Herman drove. One time we pulled over to the side for a bus. The kids had slingshots. They hit us. One time some kids threw balloons out of a car. …

"We practiced and knew what to do in case something happened. They showed us how to avoid an ambush."

Members of the One-Oh-One Airborne, as Mr. Vaughan refers to the 101st Airborne, stood shoulder to shoulder between the Little Rock Nine and the other students.

"We'd get out, walk them up to the sidewalk, walk them to the steps. A captain took them on to the school. We went back to Camp Robinson, ate lunch, returned and waited for them to get out of school."

Herman Wendell Van Patten was one of three surviving members of the six-soldier escort crew.

The number has fallen by one – Mr. Van Patten died on Saturday just when his family was breathing easy after his heart surgery in June. He was seventy-six.

Until five years ago, Mr. Van Patten's children didn't know of their father's role in Arkansas history.

"He didn't like to brag about himself," Jeff Van Patten said after the funeral service for his father at First United Methodist Church in Searcy. "I knew he was in the National Guard. I never knew he had that duty."

· · · · ·

That duty put Mr. Van Patten in the right place to extend a little humanity to one of the black youngsters, and they were young, caught in the maw of societal progress. This is what he did, the kindness he extended that bought him a reprimand: One of the Little Rock Nine girls dropped a book as she exited the brown Ford station wagon in front of Central High School.

Mr. Van Patten picked up the book and handed it back to her.

~ **July 12, 2007**

LR Nine gather for all time

On this hot August day in 2005, forty-eight years later, John Deering raised the aluminum roll-top door of the self-storage shed, and I was practically nose-to-nose with Elizabeth Eckford, she of the Little Rock Nine.

In life-size bronze as in real-life flesh, Elizabeth Eckford stood in the lead. The rest of them were there too, the other eight. We had intruded on a private gathering.

You could imagine they were frozen mid-step on a day in September 1957 and then moved into a ten-foot-by-ten-foot rented time capsule, an uncontainable moment contained for a moment.

They have been here for almost a year, created in John Deering's backyard, delivered to and then from the foundry in Santa Fe, New Mexico: Ernest Green; Melba Pattillo Beals; Elizabeth Eckford; Gloria Ray Karlmark; Carlotta Walls LaNier; Thelma Jean Mothershed; Terrence Roberts; Jefferson A. Thomas; and Minnijean Brown Trickey.

"We brought them inside every night," says John, editorial cartoonist and illustrator at the *Arkansas Democrat–Gazette*. His wife, Kathy, and a friend, Steve Scallion, helped. "At two a.m., you are surrounded by all these figures. That many people in a room — they're a presence."

Inspiration struck seven years ago, and John has found support from state Rep. Tracy Steel, state Sen. Erma Hunter Brown, and secretaries of state Sharon Priest and Charlie Daniels. The Winthrop Rockefeller Foundation and the state legislature gave the money.

On August 30, the same day the U.S. Postal Service will unveil its Little Rock Nine stamp at Central High, John will unveil his sculpture on the north side of the Capitol.

In sculpting the life-size statues, John relied on photographs, many of them by

Will Counts. The face of Elizabeth Eckford arriving for school required the least interpretation. "The photo says it all," he says. "The drama of the photo is hard to improve on."

So the bronzes stand there in the heat of the ministorage awaiting their big day, their expressions covering the gamut from worry to fright to defiance.

In the photos from those days, the anger on the faces of the teenagers in the crowd strikes me more than the faces of the Nine. I sensed, as John and I looked into the storage room, that we were part of the moment, and by extension, part of the problem. "The spectators," John observed, "sort of become the crowd."

Once installed on the concrete pad, Elizabeth Eckford will stand out front, with Ernest Green and Gloria Ray Karlmark bringing up the rear, Ernest's hand lightly on her back. "He's looking slightly behind him," John says. "Maybe he was urging her to go a little faster."

They stand there in the heat of the shade, in the heat of the shed, their names inscribed on bracelets of masking tape and string lest the installers confuse them. They wait in their temporary aluminum-sided shelter to move to their permanent pad for all of time.

John sculpted this work under the weight of history: "It has to stand the test of time."

And the work must withstand the scrutiny of those who were there, all nine of whom will be in Little Rock for the unveiling: "You want to get it right."

~ August 21, 2005

WHITE HAND, BACK POCKET

**Chapter I:
As his
mother lay
dying**

Paul Holderfield Senior found Jesus in a men's room at the old Baptist hospital, down aways from where his mother lay dying.

Any day, the doctors had been telling Paul and the rest of the family, any time.

But Paul's mother wouldn't let go. She was fretting for her son's soul. Her son, the man who was destined to become Brother Paul to a rough-tough section of North Little Rock, was still rough and rowdy himself. Paul, a cigar-chomping North Little Rock firefighter, was profane when he was drunk and profane when he wasn't, and if she wasn't there for him …

We're okay, Paul assured her. You can go on to heaven.

Who, his mother asked, is going to pray for you?

Paul, the profane alcoholic, came by it honestly. His daddy had been a drunk before him and on down the family tree. "Bub," Paul Senior would tell Paul Jr., "every Holderfield all the way back to my great-great-grandfather … they were all drunkards."

Hard times had settled in with the hard drinking. In childhood, Paul Senior had known hunger, the grocery money gone to drink. More than once, Paul and his siblings had sat at their bare supper table, their mother thanking God for the food she was certain He would provide. Later in life, Paul Senior would tell people that his family had been so poor that their rats went out to eat.

Paul Senior loved his mother, and as much as she didn't want to leave, he didn't want her to suffer. When he realized his spiritual state was the only impediment on his mother's path into eternity, he struck a deal. On that day, in the ground-floor Baptist Hospital's men's restroom, Paul Senior promised God that if He would let his mama live till Sunday, he would go to church. "That's really when he got saved," Paul Junior says. "But he thought you had to go to church."

His mother made it until Sunday. And in the car on the way home from church, Paul Senior announced his change of life. "Well, Mama,, he said to his wife, "I got to pour all my beer out."

Paul Junior, seventeen, laughed in the back seat.

"How long you think that will last?" he asked his daddy.

"Bub," his daddy replied, "I hope the rest of my life."

Eventually Paul Senior and his wife founded Friendly Chapel and opened a soup kitchen for anyone of any color. "I was hungry, and you gave Me something to eat," was a Scripture he favored from Matthew 25. "I was thirsty, and you gave Me something to drink."

Paul Senior's pledge stuck, says the junior Brother Paul: His father never drank again. Cleaned up his language too.

"When I got saved," Paul Senior would say, "I lost half my vocabulary."

And Paul Senior would say this: "A sermon heard is soon forgotten. "

"Daddy," says Brother Paul Junior, "was a sermon seen."

~ **October 30, 2008**

Chapter II: The tap of a conscience

The black hand hung there an awkward moment, suspended in a space between those two men that was close enough for a handshake but as far apart as the Selma's Edmund Pettus Bridge was long.

Paul Holderfield Senior refused the black hand. Paul Holderfield denied the man.

Paul Holderfield put his white hand in his back pocket, pretended he didn't see Jimmy Lipkin and Jimmy Lipkin's extended black hand. Jimmy Lipkin. His friend.

But Paul Holderfield saw Mr. Lipkin, all right, saw into his eyes. If betrayed was a color, that would have been the color of Mr. Lipkin's eyes.

For a long time after that, for years and years, those dark hurt eyes followed

Paul Holderfield. For years and years, Jimmy Lipkin's extended black hand tapped incessantly on Mr. Holderfield's shoulder.

• • • • •

The Holderfield brothers were a tough coupla sons of a sharecropper whose fists often spoke for them.

They grew up near Scott, trained their boxing fists at the Boy's Club, boxed their way to the Golden Gloves tournament in Chicago. Buddy Holderfield was the first brother to go, and in 1944, he won the lightweight title.

The next year, when it was Paul's turn to go, a benefactor paid Paul's bus fare to Chicago, but that didn't quite cover Paul's needs. When it was time to leave for the bus station in Little Rock, Paul didn't have the money. He was stuck in Scott.

A black sharecropper, a friend of the white Holderfield family who lived nearby, heard that Paul was stuck. He owned a car and offered the white teenage fighter a ride to town.

Jimmy Lipkin. That was the sharecropper's name.

• • • • •

Paul Holderfield lost his Golden Glove fight in Chicago in 1945. Nine years later, he hired on with the North Little Rock Fire Department.

He was twenty-five years old when the trouble erupted at Central High in 1957. National Guard troops often marched past the firehouse on their way to the school. The firefighters would shout encouragement to the soldiers, goading them to get those black troublemakers, except "black troublemakers" is not the word the firefighters used.

"We hated them," Mr. Holderfield told a reporter years later.

One day as the firefighters cheered on the troops, Mr. Holderfield noticed Jimmy Lipkin out on the street, the same kind sharecropper who a dozen years earlier had helped Paul Holderfield out of a tight spot, gave him a lift from Scott to the bus station in Little Rock.

Mr. Holderfield pretended not to see Mr. Lipkin, tried to turn so that his old friend wouldn't see him. But

Jimmy Lipkin wouldn't take the hint. Mr. Lipkin saw Mr. Holderfield, all right, and he threaded his way through the angry (un)civil servants and reached out his black hand to Mr. Holderfield.

Which is the moment that Mr. Holderfield jammed his white hand into his back pocket.

· · · · ·

Tap. Tap.
That black hand on that white shoulder.

Eighteen years later, Paul Holderfield Senior had become the Rev. Paul Holderfield, or Brother Paul, as members of his church, the Friendly Chapel, called him. Saved by the blood of Jesus in the Baptist Hospital men's room. Sober. Cigar-free.

He often told, often with tears, of the moment he betrayed Jimmy Lipkin. Paul Holderfield assumed that after all those years, Mr. Lipkin was dead.

One day, however, when he told the story to a black congregation, a woman recognized the man in the story.

What's his name? she asked.
Jimmy Lipkin, he told her.
He's not dead, she said. *He lives out in Dixie.*
Tap. Tap. Tap.

· · · · ·

1957.
1975.
White hand on the front door.
Tap. Tap.
A black woman opens the door.
Mrs. Lipkin, asks Brother Paul, *is Jimmy home?*

· · · · ·

Brother Paul apologized that day, and in the sacred quiet of repentance and reconciliation, Mr. Holderfield surrendered his hand to the grip he had refused in 1957.

Weeks later, Mr. Lipkin sat at the front of the church as Brother Paul recounted their story, admitted to his flock his public betrayal of a man who had been nothing to him but kind. And after his conversion, the memory of that sin, Brother Paul said, the fact of it, was part of the call to open this inner-city interracial branch of the Church of the Nazarene.

"Jimmy had more to do with starting this church than I did," Brother Paul said.

The two men at the front of the church moved in close then, as reporter Bill Husted wrote in the October 12, 1975, issue of the *Arkansas Democrat*. The white Mr. Holderfield draped his arm over the black Mr. Lipkin's shoulder.

"And Holderfield," Mr. Husted wrote, "stretched out his hand to Lipkin."

~ November 9, 2008

Chapter III: The other man's son

He arrived unannounced at the newspaper building. He was there for me, on a mission that required a measure of courage. He didn't know me. Had no clue how I would react to what he needed to say.

He was sitting at the round table at the top of the steps in the lobby. Security at the front desk had telephoned to tell me I had a visitor. I approached hesitantly. Didn't know him, nor of course, did I know why he was there.

He stood, a slender fellow, his beard salted and thin, stood rather quickly and leaned toward me. He spilled his words as if he were afraid I might not stay to listen.

I caught only an occasional word, so distracted was I trying to place his face, trying to discern whether this was a friendly visit.

In the midst of the tumble of his words, he said a name that I recognized. I relaxed enough to comprehend that he wanted to tell me something of importance about his daddy.

The man was Earnest Lipkin, son of Jimmy Lipkin, and he wanted to talk about the Reverend Paul Holderfield Senior. They had read my stories about Brother Paul's refusal to shake his father's hand in 1957.

Both men are dead. Their sons remain to speak for them. Earnest Lipkin wanted to offer his family's perspective.

We went for hot beverages in a hotel restaurant. We sat side by side in chairs, not across the linen-covered table from each other. His hat was summer straw, one a golfer might wear, high at the back, sloping into a jaunty bill.

He leaned to his right, shortening the distance between our faces.

"The family just wants to make sure people know there ain't no hard feelings," said Earnest, who had taken his coffee in a Styrofoam cup. "We want closure, you know."

As a child, Earnest, now seventy-two, often shared a meal at the Holderfield table, and he was a friend of brothers Buddy and Paul, the Golden Glove boxers. His daddy was the reason Paul made it to Chicago for his boxing match.

All is forgiven. Was forgiven, apparently, the moment it happened.

"Paul Senior spoke at my mama and daddy's funerals," Earnest says. "That's what our family wanted. We don't have animosity. My daddy never mentioned that [encounter] until Paul came to the house. Daddy didn't even remember him putting his hand in his pocket."

~ **November 23, 2008**

The fallen Arkansas Gazette

The *Arkansas Gazette* building looks the way a newspaper building ought to look — graceful, elegant, stately, eternal, poetic, cathedral — as if streets of gold should lead to its front door.

It looks like a building where newspaper people would do all the things you think newspaper people ought to do — the romance of the clackety presses and the world-saving you see in movies.

It is an edifice worthy of its mission, of its legacy.

How could a newspaper that lived in such a building not be great? How could someone who is called into the newspaper profession walk through the *Gazette*'s arched entrance without feeling elevated, invincible, significant?

It's a solid concrete building that, if it could wonder, would wonder at what has become of itself.

In spite of its glory, the building was on the losing end of The War. Many newspaper people in this town still think of the epic battle between the *Gazette* and the *Arkansas Democrat* as frequently as Southerners refer to that other War.

Long before I lived here, I worked at other newspapers with a few people who had worked at the *Gazette*: Maria Henson, who left here and won a Pulitzer Prize in Kentucky; Scott Morris; Craig Durrett; Michael Arbanas; Scott Stroud; Jacalyn Carfagno. They loved their newspaper, and to this day, at least one in that number won't utter the name of the *Democrat*, and the thought of working in this building — of soiling his hands, his very soul — for the enemy is anathema.

I love the sight of that old building, which is on the National Register of Historic Places, and I like to imagine my friends coming and going through the arched entrance, framed by Ionic columns, during their times here.

"A narrow band of terra-cotta fretwork runs around those sides between the first and second stories," according to a 1976 *Gazette* story. "Two-story, three-sided bays, with windows on each side, mark the top two stories, with the spaces between the second- and third-story windows decorated with terra-cotta fruit clusters.

"Miniature Doric columns separate the windows, and fluted Ionic columns separate the bays. ... On the cornice of the building is a terra-cotta lion's head."

Now the building has a new mission, as home to three charter schools, whose mission is not all that different from a newspaper's.

So as *Democrat–Gazette* employees cleaned out the basement a few weeks ago, I toured the building from the basement to the third floor. Even in the transition between missions — its floors dusty, wires dangling from the ceiling as if its guts had been ripped out in the battle — the *Gazette* building is stately.

I felt like a trespasser, and wondered how this building's former occupants would feel to know that employees of the victor's paper were intruding. I imagine some will resent someone like me, who wasn't even here for the war, presuming to write about this place. And right they would be.

I fancied the building a fallen giant, lying mortally wounded at the corner of Louisiana and Third.

In Arkansas, the *Gazette* was — is — bigger than life and beloved. Many still refer to the hyphenated survivor simply as the *Gazette*, some by habit, others in defiance.

To the winner go the spoils, and thus the ownership and now the use of the body has changed. But the building still tells of the spirit, cut asunder like a soul freed from its body of clay to float unfettered over this place.

~ **February 3, 2008**

A reluctant ex-Gazetteer

Nothing good, nothing good at all, could come out of that newspaper building around the corner, home of the archenemy *Arkansas Democrat*. That's what the soldiers in the trenches believed.

Lucifer's minions toiled in there, according to the head Gannettoids at the *Arkansas Gazette*, and so evil were they, that Al Capone looked like Mister Rogers by contrast.

So no one should have been surprised at the depth of mistrust and anger in the hearts of many Gazetteers as the newspaper war ended in the defeat of Arkansas' Old Gray Lady. You could have predicted the Gazetteers' inner conflict when their choice was to work for the enemy or unemployment.

In Sloane Cox, however, there was no ambivalence. "Do what you have to do," she told members of her sales staff on the day the *Arkansas Gazette* closed, "but I'm not going to work for them."

At twenty-eight, Sloane was one of the managers of the *Gazette's* retail advertising-sales department and one of the Gazetteers the *Democrat* hoped to hire. Without a moment's pause, however, Sloane turned down the offer flat. John Mobbs, the *Democrat's* director of advertising, approached her as she carried a box out of her office that last dark day, and she shook her head in refusal.

"Call me if you change your mind," Mr. Mobbs told her.

• • • • •

Sloane Cox, a native of DeWitt and a former Miss Arkansas County, was one of the many Gazetteers who had stayed aboard until the *Gazette's* final gasp.

Early on the Friday morning that turned out to be the *Gazette's* last, advertising managers, in an effort to prop up morale, had set up a bust-the-balloons-with-a-dart board game and awarded prizes such as *Gazette* coffee cups and T-shirts. "We knew the end was near," she says. "We had no idea it was that close."

A salesperson, with a customer on hold, asked whether she could accept an ad for the Sunday newspaper. "The management team," Sloane says, "was told to say, 'Yes, it's business as usual.'"

Late Friday morning, management summoned all employees to the newsroom, but the call was premature, and someone in management told the employees to return to work.

Few, however, were inclined to leave the newsroom, which was filled beyond its fire-marshall capacity. *Gazette* stalwarts such as Leroy Donald took to the microphone, which had been put in place for the big announcement, and told Aggie jokes and newspaper war stories.

"People were introducing themselves to familiar faces they'd seen in the hall every day for years, people they had shared an elevator with or sat near in the breakroom but didn't know."

Finally, the *Gazette's* brass appeared in the newsroom. *The* Arkansas Gazette, announced Moe Hickey, head Gannettoid at the newspaper, *has ceased publication.* Paul Smith, then vice-president of the *Arkansas Democrat*, took to the microphone. The Gazetteers, who no doubt thought they sniffed a whiff of sulfur on Paul, booed and hissed. (Paul, who retired in March 2014, came to the *Democrat* with Walter Hussman Jr. in the 1970s and was an energetic and faithful general in the war.)

After the speeches of concession and victory, Martha Jean McHaney, the *Gazette's* director of personnel, passed out the severance paperwork. People cried. And hugged. And lamented that the *Gazette* would not be publishing a farewell edition.

Pat Kiel, Sloane's boss, who was pregnant out to here and already out on maternity leave, showed up for the meeting in flipflops. Afterwards, she invited Sloane and a handful of others into her office, where she informed them that the *Democrat* wanted to hire them.

"About that time," Sloane says, "John Mobbs walked past Pat's first-floor window with a walkie-talkie in his hand. I thought he looked like a funeral director. Black suit. Somber. I was thinking, 'That's gotta be tough to look somber when you really want to celebrate.'

"He came in and passed out letters with job offers. No one, as I recall, accepted right away. He told us we could have time to think about it."

Sloane didn't need any time to think it over nor did she take any. Do what you have to do ... , she said.

At the candle-light vigil that night, Sloane was among several who delivered spirited speeches in praise of all who had labored to keep the *Gazette* alive.

And then she moved on in a career that took her to four other states, with stops at newspapers in Mobile, Alabama; Monroe, Louisiana; Chattanooga, Tennessee; and Memphis.

• • • • •

If you change your mind, John Mobbs had said. Well, Sloane did change her mind, but it happened slowly over sixteen years.

The first sign of her renewed perspective was that she actually would read the newspaper when she was back home, actually allow the ink to soil her fingers. She showed her growing, if begrudging, admiration for newly hyphenated *Democrat-*

Gazette by adapting some of its advertising ideas at the papers where she worked.

Then she took a step she never imagined: She went to work for the *Chattanooga Times-Free Press*, which Walter Hussman, the so-called and legendary Dark Knight of the *Democrat*, had purchased by then.

"It was," Sloane marvels now, "the best company I had ever worked for."

During her time in Chattanooga, she made the acquaintance of Paul Smith and Walter Hussman Jr. And of John Mobbs. To her surprise, they were all nice. Helpful. Great work ethic and high standards. The opposite of what she had come to believe during the war.

In 2007, Paul Smith recruited her to take a job as director of a newly formed department at the *Arkansas Democrat-Gazette*. Her meeting with Paul and Walter Hussman in Paul's office was surreal. She confessed that she once had loved to hate the *Democrat*. Now, however, she knew that the outcome had been the best for Arkansas. The state newspaper remained in the hands of Arkansans.

She accepted the job. Her new perspective led to some poignant moments and important events. On her first day at the *Democrat-Gazette*, she returned to the *Gazette* building to pick out make-do furniture to use until her new furniture arrived.

She toured the entire building, basement to third floor, with a stop at her former office, surprised that she was there, and even more surprised that she was furnishing an office in the building of the former competition with furniture from its fierce though fallen foe.

In the years since has returned to Little Rock, she has watched her twins, Rachel and Ryan, accept awards in the corridor that the eSTEM charter school has dubbed the Historic Hallway, where the *Gazette's* Pulitzers once hung.

She has returned to the *Gazette* building to enthrall her children's schoolmates about the building's history. She has joined the twins and their classmates at the Meet Me at the Pole prayer event on the school's playground, which once was the parking lot where she often parked her car.

On an evening in October 2011, as she waited for Rachel to finish an eSTEM basketball meeting, Sloane realized that she was at the very spot where twenty years to the day earlier, she had bid the *Gazette* and her fellow Gazetteers farewell.

In a note she to Paul Smith the next day, Sloane wrote: "I was parked in front of the building. I was looking at the front steps, and I was waiting for my daughter to walk out the same door that twenty years earlier I had walked out for what I thought was the last time. …

"I stood on those steps and delivered one of the many speeches that night to eulogize the *Gazette* before a grief-stricken crowd. I was really proud to see my daughter walk out of that school."

And she wrote words that once she couldn't have fathomed possible: She was proud of the *Democrat-Gazette* and proud to work there.

For nearly seven years, now, Sloane has traveled the city and the state, persuading the advertising community that the *Arkansas Democrat-Gazette* and *Arkansas Life* magazine are the best publications in which to spread their message.

For six years, before John Mobbs retired, Sloane worked alongside him. In his smile, and in his blue eyes, she saw the face he couldn't reveal that day he showed up at the *Gazette* dressed in black. They have talked about that difficult day, and

John and others have told her that although they were happy about their victory, their happiness was fraught with the knowledge that The War might have gone the other way.

Sloane is not the only ex-Gazetteer, of course, who has taken this path. Many have worked all over the newspaper office at Scott and Capitol, and at the printing plant the *Gazette* built.

But Sloane's is the story I know best.

In what may be the most unlikely turn of events in her life, Sloane found true love in the building she thought she never would enter. She of the *Democrat-Gazette's* advertising department married a fellow from upstairs in the *Democrat-Gazette's* newsroom.

Her reversal is complete. She is a business-card-carrying employee of the *Democrat-Gazette*, the enemy camp where her twenty-eight-year-old self was certain nothing good could exist. And now she shares the last name of a man she met at that newspaper she once so despised.

He, by the way, is me.

Griffin Smith, who resigned from the Arkansas *Democrat-Gazette* in 2012, two months shy of his twentieth anniversary as the newspaper's executive editor, knows meat and loves barbecue. (Such the connoisseur is he that he knows when a waiter has delivered to his table a different cut of meat than he ordered.) Shadden's reputation lured him and his wife, Libby, to Marvell.

After failing to find Shadden's in Marvell proper, Griffin, whose aversion to asking for directions overpowers even his love for barbecue, which is saying something, turned toward home. He accidentally found the store a few miles outside of town. But it sure didn't match his expectation.

"We went in there, it was around the lunch hour, probably a quarter to one, a time a barbecue place would be packed," he recalled in an interview in February 2014. But the legendary Shadden's looked empty, of customers at least, though not of the appliances and wall-hangings common to hundred-year-old grocery stores.

The old-fashioned meat counter with the sloping glass was slightly stocked and didn't improve his optimism about lunch. He saw a woman on the opposite side of the store. "Is this the barbecue place?" he asked.

Upon her affirmation, he said: "I would like a sliced-pork sandwich."

She went to the slightly stocked meat counter and pulled out a pork shoulder, which further dismayed our adventurer, who was accustomed to finding piles of steaming pork sliced and beckoning from a cutting board.

"This was like a piece of cold meat I was getting," he says.

Sauce on your sandwich? she asked Griffin. He declined, explaining that he preferred to sample a new barbecue without the sauce.

From a darker side of the store, Griffin heard the voice of a man he hadn't noticed. The voice offered words that changed his life. "It was one old guy, a grizzled farmer, sitting at a table ten feet away, munching on something," Griffin says.

This is what the man said: Get the sauce.

Griffin, as true to his Southern raising as he was his genetic aversion for soliciting directions, didn't want to offend the man. So against his tradition, Griffin allowed the sauce.

Still not confident, the Smiths asked to have their sandwiches wrapped to go, in case the sandwich was as bad as he was expecting. "I wanted to position myself so I didn't have to eat the whole thing in front of them." Or eat the whole thing anywhere. He was thinking he might take that first bite and toss the sandwich out the car window.

In the sanctity of their automobile, Griffin unwrapped his sandwich, found that the sauce had warmed it up and partook: "It was an epiphany," he says. "That was the magic. I tell you, we didn't waste any of it.

"The sauce made it hot and wonderful and drippy and all the magic that made Shadden's a mecca. But a strange mecca, because there weren't many pilgrims there."

No boil, no bagel

If the baker who baked your bagel didn't kettle his dough before he baked it, you didn't eat a bagel.

You ate plain ol' bread.

Or in the words of Jay Ramsey, a bagel trailblazer: "It's just a roll with a hole."

To "kettle" a bagel means to boil it in a kettle.

Boiling begets bonafide bagels.

The concept is counterintuitive. Bread in water goes soggy. Bonafide bagels are anything but soggy. And I long have wanted to understand this matter.

West of the East Coast, and south of the Northeast — outside, in other words, of the Bagel Belt, of which New York is the buckle — bonafides and their bakers are rare.

For a few years, Mr. Ramsey filled the void in these parts. He attended a university in Stillwater, Oklahoma, the unlikely birthplace of New York Bagel, which two bagel-starved students from New York founded. Mr. Ramsey worked for the company and opened a New York Bagel here in 1994. He quit making bagels two years ago.

A year ago, Roxane and David Tackett stepped into the void. They understand that Arkansas has gone cosmopolitan — Ted Danson, for crying out loud, lives in downtown Little Rock — and needs boiled bagels.

They have opened a shop in a strip center on the morning side of Maumelle Boulevard near its intersection with Counts Massie.

Roxanne dreamed up that — morning side. She insisted they open their shop on the side of Maumelle Boulevard that Maumellians travel in the morning — easy access.

And so they named their shop Morningside Bagels, "Each Batch From Scratch."

Mr. Ramsey sold some of his equipment to the Tacketts and lent them Victor, his bagel maker,.

They opened a year ago in September. This week, I found the gumption to arise at two-thirty a.m. so I could learn how to boil bread without making it soggy.

The Tacketts both make bagels, but Mrs. Tackett's cousin, David Prindle, is the head bagel maker. As Mr. Prindle worked, Mr. Tackett explained.

Mr. Priindle, following the recipe that Mr. Ramsey supplied, dumped ingredients into a bathtub-size mixer. The rest of the process is highly entertaining. If you are interested, go watch it for yourself through the window that opens into their kitchen.

But to the (boiling) point: The dough contains yeast, and Mr. Prindle allows the yeast to rise for twenty minutes, then stores them in a walk-in cooler, where they proof for at least four hours.

Then he drops the rings of dough in the kettle filled with boiling water. The hot water reactivates the yeast and creates a skin on the dough. The skin traps the gas from the yeast, and the bagels rise.

He boils them for a few seconds and bakes them for thirty minutes. Uneventful.

A letdown.

But then …

Across the kitchen from where I stood, Mr. Prindle removed the rack of two-hundred-fifty boiled and baked bagels from the oven.

Suddenly an explosion, a pleasant assault on unsuspecting senses. An infusion of moist blanketing warmth, the perfume of hot yeast, a grandmother's kitchen. A transporting moment ephemeral and eternal. Baked and boiled. No rolls with holes.

And at that moment, somewhere in cosmopolitan downtown Little Rock, Ted Danson stirred in his sleep.

How do you spell three-year-old?

At three years and eleven months of age, my Rebekah already is spelling.

"No," she exclaims to her sister. "E-R-N, No."

She's also taken up a foreign language.

"E-R-N," she says. "That says 'no' in Spanish."

As an accomplished speller, she's asserting her

independence. (Actually, this is not a new development. She came that way.) "Do your mama and daddy let you have tea?" her Aunt Julie asks.

"They're not here," she informs my sister.

She's theological. One day she learned from a Bible verse that said God makes our hearts clean. "Does that mean God licks it?" she asks, not illogically.

She's sensitive: "He hit me so hard he knocked my spirit out of me. And that hurt my feelings so badly."

She's original. After sneezing on a Christmas present she was wrapping, she says: "I achooed on that."

She's creative. One day in the car, she's reporting that she sees something interesting in the clouds.

"What do you see?"

"A tongue," she says.

"Is it attached to anything?"

"A dog," she says.

And some days she is real creative. One day after a discussion about a man smoking a cigarette, Rebekah said: "I saw a baby smoking a cigarette one day. It looked so silly I couldn't believe it."

She's sounding like a teenager: "Could I, like, have some cover here? I'm cold."

Or, referring to the car's air conditioning: "Could I, like, have some cold stuff back here? I'm hot."

She's already trying to neaten my appearance. "I'm going to fix you a hair-dude," she says, coming at me with a comb.

She's loving and spontaneous, the nicest baby a parent could want, right up there with her big sister.

On Christmas morning, she opened a present her big sister had given her. It was her sister's prized "Nutcracker" doll. Rebekah had fallen in love with it, and Samantha decided to surprise her with it as a Christmas gift.

Samantha and Rebekah were sitting side by side. When Rebekah opened it and saw what was inside, she looked as if she might cry.

At three, Rebekah understood the gift. On her knees, without prompting from and without saying a word, she went to her big sister, laid her head on her shoulder and wrapped her up in a hug.

It was one of those moments. My throat tightened and my heart palpitated. I was awash in gratitude for the love that fills our lives. Something slid out of the corner of my eyes. My children call them happy tears. E-R-N. Happy tears.

From the Gazette to UPI and back

JFK rose from his seat on the podium, then Willie Allen stood, and Willie was face to face with the president, his camera the only thing between them.

John Fitzgerald Kennedy stood at the lectern, well-spoken, his pauses perfectly timed. Self-deprecating. Hours from eternity.

Willie Allen raised his camera and made his pictures — young Willie from North Little Rock, who bluffed his way into his first job as a newspaper photographer at the *Arkansas Gazette*. Willie, UPI photographer, the kid from Arkansas, occupying a front-row seat to history.

Young Willie Allen took his pictures, unaware that history would inscribe them as photos of the last speech of President Kennedy's life.

• • • • •

Willie Allen was a part-timer in 1957, writing high school sports stories for the *Arkansas Gazette*, when a photography job opened up.

"The managing editor, Nelson, he was a crusty old character," Willie recalls. "I was afraid to go talk to him."

But not too afraid to pad his resume when Mr. Nelson asked about his experience.

He had been a photographer for his high school yearbook, Willie bluffed.

"I lied," says Willie, who still makes money taking pictures in Little Rock. "I'd never had a camera in my hand."

The desegregation of Central High was Willie's first big story. In 1960, *Gazette* editors sent him to Los Angeles to cover the Democrats' presidential convention, where UPI editors offered him a job.

"How soon can you be in Austin?" the editor-in-chief asked.

Two years later, UPI moved Willie to from Austin to Dallas, where he was posted on November. 22, 1963.

• • • • •

Willie started his day photographing JFK's brief impromptu speech in a drizzle outside the Hotel Texas, where the Kennedys had spent the night. Then Willie followed the president inside for his speech to Texas Democrats.

Willie stayed just long enough to take a couple of photos, then returned to the Dallas Times-Herald, where he worked for that paper under an agreement with UPI.

Willie developed the film, printed the pictures, sent them out on the UPI wire and was dashing to catch up with JFK when the city editor shouted: "Get to the triple underpass. There's been a homicide."

Willie ran out the building.

The Dallas Times-Herald building was two blocks from the Texas Book Depository, which is near the triple underpass.

Willie took pictures of the window where minutes earlier the killer had fired his rifle. Willie ran into the Texas School Book Depository while, unbeknownst to Willie, Mr. Oswald was still inside.

Before the day was over, Willie photographed the bump that history would describe as the Grassy Knoll and took pictures of Mr. Oswald as police hauled him to headquarters.

"We worked two or three days without going home," he says. "We'd sleep on sofas in the women's restroom. It was unbelievable, not knowing what was going on, what was going to happen next."

On Sunday, November 24, police prepared to move the accused assassin from the city jail. Willie's assignment was to photograph Mr. Oswald as police arrived with him at the county jail.

"It was going to be so simple," Willie says, "moving him six blocks."

Mr. Allen, waiting store on the route by which Mr. Oswald would be escorted, watched the transfer on a television. When Jack Ruby stepped into the picture and shot Mr. Oswald, Willie hot-footed it back to the Dallas Times-Herald building.

Bob Jackson, assigned to the city jail, had been directly in front of Mr. Oswald when Jack Ruby shot him. Mr. Jackson ran into the newsroom, shaken and nervous. He knew he had fired his camera. He didn't know what his film had captured.

Willie went into the darkroom with him and viewed the developed film as it came out of the chemicals. "The first exposure was typical," Willie says.

The second exposure more typical.

"The third exposure," Willie says, "Ruby stepped out and shot."

The image they watched develop would become the historic and iconic photograph of the shooting.

• • • • •

Seven people entered Jack Ruby's apartment that night forty-five years ago:

Jack Ruby's roommate. A couple of attorneys. A Los Angeles Times reporter. Two reporters from the Dallas Times-Herald. And Willie Allen.

Mr. Allen, who grew up in North Little Rock, was armed with a camera. And the assignment earned him a mention in the Warren Commission report about the assassination of John Fitzgerald Kennedy.

Mr. Allen knew Jack Ruby before the rest of the world knew him. Mr. Allen occasionally photographed dancers for the marquee on Mr. Ruby's nightclub.

"Ruby was a likeable guy," says Mr. Allen, who lives east of Little Rock and still earns a living with his camera. "He'd come up to the office and try to sell us watches."

The contents of Jack Ruby's apartment, Willie says, had been tossed and overturned, he says, "just like a movie."

The Dallas Times-Herald and UPI published his photographs, which is how his name ended up in the Warren report.

Gary Mack — curator of the Sixth Floor Museum at Dealey Plaza, which collects assassination material — is very familiar with Willie's photographs from that weekend.

"One of the Allen pictures in Ruby's apartment actually shows the newspaper Ruby was reading when he left," Mr. Mack says. "It includes the 'Letter to Caroline' that may have been one of the emotional triggers that led Ruby to shoot Oswald."

• • • • •

Before I ever heard of Willie Allen, I knew about one of his photographs, one that is famous, at least with local news people. He took a picture of the late John Robert Starr, then the managing editor of the Arkansas Democrat, that showed Starr crouching on an *Arkansas Gazette* newspaper box with a knife in his mouth and declaring war. The Arkansas Times, which was a monthly magazine then, published the picture on its cover in May 1979.

Willie is one of many Arkansans who started his news career in Arkansas then left to pursue big-city journalism. And Willie is one of the few who returned here to live.

• • • • •

A lot of people knew Lyndon Baines Johnson. Few, though, knew LBJ well enough to take a picture of him in his night clothes.

Willie Allen did.

Of all the famous, infamous and important people Willie met in his time as a UPI photographer in Texas, the famous person Willie knew the best was LBJ.

By the time Willie moved to Texas, Senator Johnson was the vice-presidential nominee. Willie was with LBJ in his Austin apartment on the night he was elected.

Willie once toured LBJ's ranch in a convertible Lincoln, with the vice president at the wheel. "He drove it like a Jeep," Willie recalls.

Willie knew LBJ well enough that the vice president didn't bother to dress when Willie and his Leica 35-millimeter camera arrived. LBJ's only restriction was that Willie never photograph him wearing his reading spectacles.

One morning, Willie disregarded the vice president's wishes.

"I walk in. LBJ had on his pajamas and a robe and his Ben Franklin glasses. He sat down and was reading the paper. My Leica was pretty quiet."

Willie sneaked two pictures but to make certain he had a good picture, he shot one more.

"The third shot, he heard it," Mr. Allen says, at which time the vice president unloosed a stream of the profanities for which he was famous.

"If I told you once,'" Mr. Allen recalls that LBJ hollered between oaths, "'I told you a dozen times.'"

And then the vice president confiscated the evidence.

"He made me give him the film," Mr. Allen says. "I had to take the film out of the camera."

I am closing in on eleven years in Arkansas, the longest I've stayed in one place since I left home for Louisiana Tech. I harbor neither plan nor desire to live anywhere else. I have worked at good newspapers in interesting places: *The Alexandria* (Louisiana) *Daily Town Talk; The Palm Beach Post; The Shreveport Times; The Baton Rouge Morning Advocate; The Denver Post; The Lexington* (Kentucky) *Herald-Leader; Mobile* (Alabama) *Register; The Oklahoman*; and *The Sun-News* in Myrtle Beach, South Carolina. My first byline was in the weekly *Red River Journal*. I left the *Democrat-Gazette* and daily newspapers in September 2013 to do all those things I've prattled on about all of my adult life. *Sweet Tea Times* is the first project. I don't call my little enterprise the Storytelling, Sweet Tea and Housewashing Society for nothing. (I will tell your story, sell you a story, cater your event with my homemade sweet tea or wash your house. Or all of the above. Write to the P.O. Box on the copyright page.) Think of my adventure as Charles Kuralt Washes America. Or at least Arkansas.

The good you see in *Sweet Tea Times* is thanks to the folks who worked so hard with me, the mistakes, mine. David Bailey, *Democrat-Gazette* managing editor, hired me and turned me loose in Arkansas. As deadline approached, David would appear, his left arm crooked, and patiently tap his watch with his right index finger. Some days, Mr. Bailey collared Danny Shameer, now city editor, to wrestle the column out of me. Eventually, Alyson Hogue rescued our boss and took charge of me. The *Democrat-Gazette* copy desk suffered through the newspaper version of these. I convinced my mother to copy edit an early version of this project. My sister Julie designed the book and did all the technical work, which cost her much sleep.

Sloane, my brown-eyed girl and wife, without whom none of the joys of my life would be possible …. There is no end to the love, energy and skill she poured into this project and pours into my life. She has given me the freedom to pursue this. She loves me enough to fly alongside me.

But they that wait upon the LORD shall renew their strength; they shall mount up with wings as eagles; they shall run, and not be weary; and they shall walk, and not faint. Isaiah 40:31

This is part index and part advertisement, a coming-soon-to-a-book near-you announcement, if you will. As I sifted through the thousand or so columns that I wrote for the Arkansas Democrat-Gazette *for the first edition of* Sweet Tea Time*s, I ran out of time and space. I realized that I have stories enough and more for at least one more volume.*